ALL-STAR **REAL FOOD** COOKBOOK

100 favorite recipes from the biggest names in health!

FOREWORD
BY BOBBI BROWN

Beauty is not just what you put on your face, it's what you put in your body.

Eating whole foods nourishes your body and ultimately shows on your face. Brighter eyes and smooth skin are the results of good lifestyle habits and real food.

As a beauty expert and a health coach, I know first hand how important it is to eat well. When I don't, I look and feel instantly worse, and it reminds me to get back to a better lifestyle. Making changes to your diet is a journey.

When you start to notice how much better you feel eating real foods it becomes easier, and a new norm. Opt for things that grow from the ground and not in a factory. Learn new ways to make food taste good. That's exactly what this book will teach you.

The *All-Star Real Food Cookbook* makes eating well, simple. It has a collaboration of wellness experts showing you what they eat, and they teach you how to do the same. Experts like Mark Sisson, Robb Wolf, Dr. Terry Wahls and more give you a peek into their kitchens and give you inspiration for new ways of eating.

From sliders to soups to an easy kale salad or grilled fish, the recipes are delicious, easy, and accessible. Food is meant to be enjoyed and shared. Get ready to be inspired and educated.

Bobbi Brown

Paleo Treats Inc
941 Orange Ave, #302
Coronado CA 92118

Ordering Information: Quantity sales. Special discounts are available on quantity purchases by corporations, associations, and others. For details, contact the publisher at the address above.

Orders by U.S. trade bookstores and wholesalers. Please contact Paleo Treats Inc:
visit paleotreats.com

First paperback edition October 2019

Book design by Paleo Treats Inc

ISBN 978-0-578-50666-1

www.paleotreats.com

Printed in USA

INTRO

Thank you so much for picking up the *All-Star Real Food Cookbook*. Lee & I are excited to be sharing some of our favorite recipes and recipe creators with you! In 10+ years of being on clean food and real food diets, we've found that you have to explore a lot of "food territory" to find what works best for you.

Throughout our explorations we've met all kinds of passionate and REALLY capable chefs: Paleo, keto, gluten free, vegan, AIP, lactose-free. Each chef has found a diet and recipes that work for them. We are so happy to be sharing the results of these explorations with you.

Food is an important part of a healthy life, and different diets work for different people. There is not one perfect diet. YOU have to find what works for YOU!

In here you'll find all kinds of real food recipes; no need for fancy ingredients, synthetic stabilizers, or preservatives. Our goal is to provide you with a stable of great recipes that meet your needs and that you can rely on to help you meet your goals, whether they be dietary, performance, weight loss, or even clear thinking.

You'll see that each chef has a slightly different take on food, from how they measure to how they make their favorite foods. Celebrate the differences; making food in new ways is one of the best ways to build a better understanding of the diversity in our world.

Here's to great tasting clean food and your health!

Nik & Lee
Owners of Paleo Treats
Editors, All Star Real Food Cookbook

Table of Contents

Pictured on front cover: Korean Rice Bowl
by Dr. Kellyann Petrucci (page 122)

Table of Contents

Diane SANFILIPPO

BALANCED BITES FOUNDER

Diane Sanfilippo is the owner and founder of Balanced Bites, a certified Nutrition Consultant, and two-time *New York Times* best-selling author of *Practical Paleo*, and The *21-Day Sugar Detox* series and co-author of *Mediterranean Paleo Cooking*. Her most recent book is *Keto Quick Start*, which released January 1, 2019.

Diane holds a BS from Syracuse University and is certified in holistic nutrition, holistic lifestyle coaching, and Poliquin BioSignature Modulation. She is the co-creator of the Balanced Bites Master Class, the co-host of the top-rated health podcast *The Balanced Bites Podcast*, and co-host of the brand-new entrepreneurial podcast, *Driven*. She is also the creator of *Balanced Bites Spices & Meals*.

Diane lives in San Francisco with her husband, Scott, and two fur kids.

www.balancedbites.com

/thediesanfilippo @dianesanfilippo

RECIPES

Chicken Satay Sandwiches with Blistered Peppers

Dairy-Free Spinach Artichoke Dip

Dairy-Free Chocolate Mousse

Green Sauce Marinated Steak + Plantain Bowl

Meatball Sandwich Burgers with Marinara

SERVES 4

Chicken Satay Sandwiches with Blistered Peppers

At first glance, this recipe uses a lot of ingredients, but most of them are spices you likely have on hand or that are easily found in any grocery store. Stocking your pantry and fridge with a few special Paleo staples like coconut aminos and fish sauce will make cooking Asian-inspired recipes a cinch!

MARINADE

1/2 cup full-fat coconut milk

1 tsp grated or minced fresh garlic

1 tsp grated or minced fresh ginger

1 tsp turmeric powder

1/2 tsp ground coriander

1/2 tsp sea salt

1/2 tsp black pepper

1 small onion, thinly sliced, or 1 Tbsp onion powder

1 1/2 pounds boneless, skinless chicken breast, butterflied

SLAW

juice of 1 lime

2 Tbsp extra-virgin olive oil

sea salt and black pepper

1 cup thinly sliced or shredded cabbage, red or green or a combination

1/4 cup shredded carrots

SATAY SAUCE

1/2 cup almond butter, sunflower seed butter, or tahini (sesame paste), raw or roasted

1/2 cup coconut aminos

1/4 cup organic rice vinegar

a few dashes of fish sauce

1/4 tsp ground black pepper

1/4 tsp sea salt

1/4 tsp red pepper flakes

1/2 tsp toasted sesame seeds

FOR SERVING

1 head butter lettuce, separated into leaves

1 recipe Blistered Shishito Peppers (recipe below) (optional)

FOR GARNISH (OPTIONAL)

sliced red bell pepper

chopped fresh cilantro

lime wedges

In a mixing bowl, combine the ingredients for the marinade. Note that it will be a thick, more pastelike marinade rather than a more liquidy marinade. Place the chicken in the bowl and massage the marinade into it. Refrigerate for at least 20 minutes or up to overnight.

While the chicken marinates, prepare the slaw and satay sauce. To make the slaw, whisk together the lime juice, olive oil, and a few pinches each of salt and pepper in a mixing bowl, then toss the cabbage and carrots in the dressing and set aside. In a separate mixing bowl, whisk together the sauce ingredients until combined and set aside.

Preheat a grill or grill pan to medium-high heat. Grill the chicken for 4 to 5 minutes per side, depending on the thickness of the chicken, until it's white all the way through. When you notice that the chicken has turned white up around the sides and toward the middle, it's time to flip it.

To serve, place a piece of chicken on top of a lettuce leaf and top with the slaw and optional garnishes. Serve with the satay sauce and Blistered Shishito Peppers, if desired.

HOW TO MAKE BLISTERED SHISHITO PEPPERS: Toss 12 ounces of Shishito peppers (or other small peppers) in a large skillet that's been preheated over high heat with about 2 teaspoons of the cooking fat of your choice and a few pinches of sea salt. Sauté until charred, and finish with coarse sea salt before serving.

PARTY TIME! Cut chicken breast into strips or use tenders and place the pieces on skewers before marinating to grill up as single-serving bites with the sauce at a party—fun!

SERVES 3

Dairy-Free Spinach Artichoke Dip

This spinach and artichoke dip is the perfect appetizer to make for your next party. Packed with flavor and seriously simple to throw together, this dip will become one of your go-to recipes for future get-togethers! Bring it to a New Year's Eve celebration, Super Bowl Party, or even a backyard BBQ. It's sure to be a hit, I'm telling you. You can serve this dip with crudités, baked potato chips, or plantain chips.

- 1 Tbsp extra virgin olive oil
- 1 small yellow onion, chopped
- 2 large cloves garlic, grated or minced
- 1 Tbsp ghee or butter
- 1 pound frozen spinach, thawed, with the water squeezed out
- 1 (14-ounce) can artichoke hearts, chopped
- 1 tsp granulated onion
- 1/2 tsp granulated garlic
- 1/2 tsp paprika
- 2 tsp sea salt
- 1/2 tsp black pepper

ALMOND CREAM

- 1 cup blanched almond flour
- 3/4 cup hot water
- 1/2 tsp sea salt
- 1/2 cup nutritional yeast

Heat the olive oil in a medium-sized saucepan over medium heat. Add the onion and garlic and cook for 10 minutes, stirring often.

Make a well in the onion mixture and add the ghee. Once the ghee has melted, turn the heat down to medium-low and add the spinach, artichoke hearts, granulated onion, granulated garlic, paprika, salt, and pepper and stir to combine. Continue to cook for 10 minutes, stirring often.

Meanwhile, make the almond cream: Blend together the almond flour, hot water, and salt in a food processor or high-speed blender until a smooth cream forms.

Once the spinach artichoke mixture has cooked for 10 minutes, remove the pan from the heat and add the almond cream and nutritional yeast. Stir to combine.

This dip can be served warm, chilled, or at room temperature and can be reheated in a preheated 350°F oven for 10 minutes. Store leftovers in an airtight glass container for up to a week. This recipe can be made up to a few days in advance of a party.

NUT-FREE? To make this dip nut-free, make a sunflower cream instead of the almond cream. Simply blend together ¾ cup of unsweetened sunflower seed butter with ½ to ¾ cup of hot water (start with ½ cup and add more if it seems too thick) and a pinch of salt until a smooth cream forms.

SEED-FREE? For a dip that is both nut-free and seed-free, puree an avocado with ¼ cup of warm water and use it instead of the almond cream.

NIGHTSHADE-FREE? Omit the paprika.

SERVES 2

Dairy-Free Chocolate Mousse

Eliminating dairy can seem daunting when making desserts, but this avocado-based mousse is surprisingly easy to make and so delicious that you won't miss the dairy one bit.

2 ripe avocados, cut in half and pitted

1/4 cup unsweetened cacao powder

2 to 4 Tbsp full-fat coconut milk (use less milk if omitting the banana)

1 ripe banana (optional)

1 to 4 Tbsp pure maple syrup or softened honey, or to taste (omit if including the banana and it is sweet enough)

1/2 tsp pure vanilla extract

pinch of ground cinnamon

pinch of sea salt

cacao nibs, chopped toasted hazelnuts, or unsweetened shredded coconut, for garnish (optional)

Scoop the flesh of the avocados into a food processor. Add the cacao powder, coconut milk, banana (if using), maple syrup, vanilla extract, cinnamon, and salt and process until creamy, whipped, and well blended.

Serve in two individual dishes or bowls. Garnish with cacao nibs (pictured), toasted hazelnuts, or shredded coconut.

EQUIPMENT TIP If you don't have a food processor, you can use an immersion blender to whip the ingredients together.

SERVES 4-6

Green Sauce Marinated Steak + Plantain Bowl

This preparation will quickly become your favorite way to enjoy steak. It's bold and flavorful and can be used to top salads or enjoyed on its own, as in this recipe.

GREEN SAUCE MARINADE

2 Tbsp Diane's Magic Green Sauce*

1 Tbsp extra-virgin olive oil

juice of 2 limes

1/2 tsp sea salt

1/2 tsp black pepper

1/2 tsp chili powder

1/2 tsp ground coriander

1/2 tsp ground cumin

1/2 tsp paprika

2 pounds flank steak

2 red bell peppers, sliced

SAUTÉED SWEET PLANTAINS

1/2 tsp ground cinnamon

1/2 tsp paprika

1/2 tsp sea salt

1/4 tsp coconut sugar (optional)

2 black (very ripe) plantains

1/4 cup coconut oil, ghee, or butter, or more as needed

FOR SERVING

1 recipe Cilantro Cauli-Rice (optional)*

2 avocados, sliced

fresh pico de gallo, store-bought or homemade (optional)

FOR GARNISH (OPTIONAL)

chopped fresh cilantro

lime wedges

*Find this on Diane's website, www.balancedbites.com

Make the marinade: In a large glass baking dish, whisk together the green sauce, olive oil, lime juice, salt, and spices.

Marinate the steak: Place the steak in the baking dish with the marinade and massage the seasonings into it. Place in the refrigerator to marinate for at least 20 minutes or up to overnight.

When ready to grill the steak, preheat a grill or grill pan to high heat. Cook the steak for 3 to 5 minutes per side, depending on the thickness and desired level of doneness. Set the cooked steak aside to rest for 10 minutes. While the steak is resting, grill the sliced bell peppers until they are soft and have grill marks, about 5 minutes, turning as needed to prevent burning.

Make the plantains: In a small bowl, combine the cinnamon, paprika, salt, and sugar (if using); set aside. Cut the plantains on the bias into ¼-inch-thick slices.

Heat the coconut oil in a sauté pan over medium heat. Use enough oil to completely cover the bottom of the pan and come at least halfway up the sides of the plantain slices. Add the plantains in a single layer, working in batches so as not to overcrowd the pan, and cook for 3 to 4 minutes per side, until lightly browned and cooked through. The plantains are ready to flip when they release from the bottom of the pan with little resistance. Place the sautéed plantains on a plate lined with paper towels and season immediately with the spice mixture.

To serve, slice the steak against the grain into thin strips. Place the steak over the cauli-rice (if using) and add the grilled bell pepper strips, sautéed plantains, and sliced avocado. If desired, garnish with cilantro and a squeeze of fresh lime juice and enjoy with fresh pico de gallo.

SPICE BLEND SWAP Replace the salt and spices in the marinade with 1 tablespoon of Balanced Bites Taco & Fajita blend.

LOVE PLANTAINS? The sweet, ripe plantains pair perfectly with the savory spices in this dish. You can also serve these sautéed plantains with eggs and bacon or sausage for breakfast!

SERVES 4

Meatball Sandwich Burgers with Marinara

Growing up in an Italian New Jersey family meant eating meatball and eggplant sandwiches pretty often! This burger is a twist on those classics. It can easily be made without the eggplant if you want to simplify it, or you can make it more like a meatball parm sandwich by topping it with the béchamel sauce that's in the 2nd edition of Practical Paleo.

GRILLED EGGPLANT

1 medium eggplant, cut into 8 (1/2-inch) slices

1 Tbsp extra-virgin olive oil

sea salt

BURGERS

3/4 pound ground beef

3/4 pound ground pork

1/2 cup chopped fresh basil

1/4 cup chopped fresh parsley

1 tsp dried oregano leaves

1 tsp black pepper

1/2 tsp granulated garlic

1/2 tsp granulated onion

1 tsp sea salt

1 tsp almond flour

1 large egg

FOR SERVING

8 Portobello "Buns" (instructions below) or 8 large lettuce leaves for wrapping

8 large fresh basil leaves

1 cup pizza sauce or marinara (use a no-sugar-added variety), warmed

1 red onion, sliced

Preheat a grill or grill pan to medium-high heat. Brush the eggplant slices with the olive oil and sprinkle with a few pinches of salt. Grill for 5 to 6 minutes, until softened and browned with grill marks, turning as needed to prevent burning.

Prepare the portobello "buns," if using them to serve the burgers.

Make the burgers. In a large mixing bowl, combine the meat, herbs, spices, salt, almond flour, and egg; using your hands, mix everything together until well integrated. Form the meat into four 6-ounce patties, adding a thumbprint dimple in the center of each one to allow for even cooking.

Grill the burgers over medium-high heat for 5 minutes per side or until cooked to 145°F in the center.

To serve, place 2 slices of grilled eggplant in a portobello "bun" or lettuce leaf, then add a burger patty, a couple of basil leaves, ¼ cup of the pizza sauce, and a couple of slices of onion. Top with another mushroom cap or lettuce leaf.

NUT-FREE? Omit the almond flour.

EGG-FREE? Omit the egg.

FODMAP-FREE? Omit the granulated garlic and onion.

HOW TO MAKE PORTOBELLO "BUNS": On a grill or grill pan preheated to medium-high heat, grill 8 stemmed mushroom caps, "cup" side down, for about 10 minutes, until they begin to soften. You can also bake them on a rimmed baking sheet in a preheated 350°F oven for about 10 minutes.

Meatball Sandwich Burger with marinara pictured far left.

Betty ROCKER

THE BETTY ROCKER FOUNDER

Bree Argetsinger, aka The Betty Rocker is an internationally known health and fitness coach, innovative entrepreneur and motivator of self growth.

A C.H.E.K. certified exercise coach, nationally certified structural integration practitioner, and ISSA certified fitness nutrition practitioner, there's clearly more than charm behind her success. In the past 3 years, over 2 million people have taken her 30-day #makefatcry challenge, and hundreds of thousands more have done her workout and nutrition programs.

She incorporates a strong, holistic focus on body balancing, self-kindness and alignment into her fitness and nutrition programs. Hailed as a "gateway to personal growth through food and fitness" she empowers her massive worldwide audience to live a "healthy lifestyle of awesome" by teaching them to listen to their the bodies and providing them with a knowledge base from which to thrive.

www.thebettyrocker.com

/thebettyrocker   @thebettyrocker    @bettyrockershow

RECIPES

Buckwheat Bread

Chicken Nuggets

Mediterranean Chicken

Peanut Butter Chocolate Chunk Cookie Dough

Peppermint Chip Green Smoothie

SERVES 6 - 8

Buckwheat Bread

You will need: 4 mini loaf pans, measuring cups and spoons, food processor, large mixing bowl, mixing spoon.

2 1/2 cups buckwheat groats

4 cups water, divided

3 Tbsp lemon juice

1/2 cup pumpkin seeds, divided

4 Tbsp flaxseed meal, divided

1-2 tsp sea salt

Measure the groats into a bowl and cover with 3 cups of water. Add the lemon juice and stir.

Cover the mixture and set on your stovetop (or somewhere else slightly warm) for 6-8 hours.

Optional - Drain your groats and add fresh water 1-2 times during the soaking process.

After the soaking process, drain the water and rinse 1-2 times with fresh water and re-drain thoroughly.

Add 1 ⅓ cups fresh water and gently stir to combine.

Place half the mixture in your food processor and blend until smooth.

Transfer the batter to the new bowl and repeat with the remaining mixture. Add this to the bowl.

Cover the blended mixture and set aside in a warm place (67-70°F) for 24 hours. Do not mix or stir the batter during this process, as it will deflate.

Uncover the batter - you should see a darker colored outer ring due to expansion from fermentation.

Add ⅓ cup pumpkin seeds, 3 Tbsp flaxseed meal, and 1 tsp sea salt. Gently fold into the batter, but don't over-mix.

Transfer the batter evenly into the 4 mini loaf pans. Sprinkle the remaining flaxseed meal and pumpkin seeds on top.

Cover and let the batter rise for another 30-60 minutes. While the batter is rising, preheat your oven to 350°F.

Bake for 1 hour 10 minutes. Test with a toothpick inserted and visually see the bread pulling away and turning golden brown against the side edges.

Remove from the pan and cool 15-20 minutes before slicing.

SERVES 4

Chicken Nuggets

You will need: baking sheet, parchment paper, measuring cups and spoons, knife, cutting board, bowls, whisk or fork.

- 1 lb chicken breast
- 2 eggs
- 1 cup almond meal flour
- 1 cup unsweetened shredded coconut
- 1 tsp garlic powder
- 1 tsp onion powder
- sea salt and pepper to taste

Preheat the oven to 350°F. Line a baking sheet with parchment paper.

Prepare the chicken by cutting it into even, bite-sized pieces.

Set out 2 bowls. In the first bowl, beat the eggs together. In the second bowl, combine the almond meal flour, coconut, and seasonings.

Dip the chicken pieces into the egg and then dredge in the almond/coconut mixture. Lay on the baking sheet.

Bake for 20-25 minutes or until browned and cooked through.

SERVES 4

Mediterranean Chicken

You will need: baking sheet, knife, cutting board, measuring cups and spoons, fork, medium-sized pan, mixing bowl.

6 cups spaghetti squash

1 tbsp olive oil

2 tsp sea salt, divided

1 lb chicken breast (or 16 oz tempeh)

1/2 cup sun-dried tomatoes

4 small roma tomatoes, chopped

1/2 cup kalamata olives, chopped

3/4 -1 cup Perfect Pesto*

OPTIONA TOPPING

chopped fresh basil

Preheat your oven to 400°F.

Slice the spaghetti squash in half lengthwise and scoop out the seeds.

Drizzle each half with the olive oil and season with 1 tsp salt. Place the squash cut-side down on a baking sheet and roast until tender, about 45-50 minutes.

Once cooked and cooled, use a fork to scrape out the "spaghetti" and set aside.

Heat a pan to medium. Add a little olive oil to heat. Add the chicken breast (or tempeh) and 1 tsp salt. Sauté until cooked through.

Once the chicken is cooked, remove it from the heat and let it cool completely.

Add the sun-dried tomatoes, roma tomatoes, olive, and ½ of the pesto to the same pan the chicken was cooked in. Cook until warm.

Dice the cooked chicken and add it back to the pan, along with the spaghetti squash and remaining pesto.

Mix it all together and cook for 1-2 minutes, or until warm.

Top with basil and serve.

*Find Betty Rocker's Perfect Pesto on her website www.thebettyrocker.com

YIELD 12 BITES

Peanut Butter Chocolate Chunk Cookie Dough

You will need: food processor, measuring cups and spoons, rubber spatula, platter or baking sheet, parchment paper.

- 2/3 cup walnuts
- 2/3 cup almonds
- 2/3 cup flaxseed meal
- 1/4 tsp sea salt
- 3/4 tsp cinnamon
- 1/4 cup peanut butter
- 1 tsp vanilla extract
- 1/4 cup honey
- 1/4-1/2 cup cacao nibs

In a food processor, blend the walnuts, almonds, flaxseed meal, salt, and cinnamon until you've created a fine textured meal.

Add the peanut butter, vanilla, and honey - process again until combined.

Lastly, add in the cacao nibs and pulse a few times to mix.

Roll into even sized balls and place on a platter or baking sheet lined with parchment paper. Store in the refrigerator.

SERVES 1

Peppermint Chip Green Smoothie

You will need: blender, measuring cups and spoons.

- 1-2 cups/handfuls baby spinach
- 1 banana
- 1 scoop vanilla protein powder
- 1 cup almond milk (or other non-dairy milk you like)
- 1/2 tsp peppermint extract
- 2 Tbsp cacao nibs

Add everything to a blender* except the cacao nibs.

Blend very well until smooth.

Add the cacao nibs and pulse the blender briefly.

*If your blender is low-powered, you can try blending your greens and liquids first, then adding the banana and protein powder. This will result in a smoother texture.

Cain CREDICOTT

PALEO MAGAZINE FOUNDER

Cain Credicott is the founder/editor-in-chief of *Paleo Magazine*, the premiere print publication dedicated to the Paleo lifestyle and ancestral health. Since 2011, *Paleo Magazine* has been providing readers all over the world with information to help them live strong, vibrant, healthy lives. Cain is also the co-founder of Restorative Blends, a supplement company committed to providing nutritional supplements that make a positive impact on one's health and well-being, and a co-owner of Lux, a producer of CBD-infused organic nut butters.

These recipes are some of his favorites, taken from issues of *Paleo Magazine* over the past few years. Each of these is always in regular rotation in his menu at home - they are easy to make, full of flavor, and always popular with eaters both young and old.

www.paleomagazine.com

RECIPES

Avocado-Lime "Cheesecake" Tarts

Cilantro-Avocado Shrimp Salad

Garlic Topped Flank Steak Roulade

Paleo Flatbread

Salisbury Steak with Mushroom Gravy

SERVES 12

Avocado-Lime "Cheesecake" Tarts

FOR THE CRUST

2 cups unsweetened coconut flakes

1/2 cup (packed) pitted Medjool dates

2 Tbsp raw honey

1 tsp pure vanilla extract

FOR THE FILLING

2 medium-sized, ripe avocados, pitted

1/4 cup coconut oil, melted

1/4 cup raw honey

2 Tbsp fresh lime juice

2 tsp finely grated lime zest

1/2 cup unsweetened coconut flakes, for garnish

Line 12 cups of a standard muffin pan with paper liners. Set aside.

In a food processor fitted with the steel blade, combine the coconut flakes and dates. Process until finely ground, about 30 seconds. Add the honey and vanilla. Process until the mixture is well-combined and holds together when pinched between your fingers. Divide crust among the prepared muffin cups, pressing the dough firmly into the bottom of each cup.

Wipe out the food processor. Scoop the avocado flesh into the food processor. Add the coconut oil, honey, lime juice, and lime zest. Process until very smooth, stopping as needed to scrape down the sides of the bowl. Divide the mixture among the muffin cups, spreading the tops with the back of a spoon to make them level. Garnish with coconut flakes.

Freeze for 1 hour or until firm. Store in an airtight container in the freezer. Thaw at room temperature for 10 minutes before serving.

SERVES 4

Cilantro-Avocado Shrimp Salad

2/3 cup packed, fresh cilantro

1/2 cup fresh lime juice (from about 5 limes)

1/3 cup olive oil

1 Tbsp raw honey

1 tsp chili powder

1/2 tsp sea salt

1 lb large (31-40 count) shrimp, peeled and deveined

6 cups chopped romaine lettuce

1 cup thinly sliced red cabbage

1 cup cherry tomatoes, halved

2 ripe avocados, peeled, pitted, and diced

To make the dressing, place the cilantro, lime juice, olive oil, honey, chili powder, and salt in a blender or food processor. Blend until fairly smooth.

Place the shrimp in a zip-top bag and add about ⅓ cup of the dressing. Reserve the remaining dressing for the salad. Mix to combine, seal the bag, and refrigerate for 30-60 minutes.

Heat a grill to medium-high heat. Remove the shrimp from the marinade and thread onto grilling skewers. Oil the grill grates. Grill the shrimp for 2-3 minutes. Flip and continue grilling for an additional 2-3 minutes, or until cooked throughout.

In a large bowl, combine the romaine, cabbage, and tomatoes. Toss with the reserved dressing. Add the grilled shrimp and avocados, and toss gently to combine. Serve immediately.

SERVES 4

Garlic Topped Flank Steak Roulade

ROULADE

2 pounds flank steak

sea salt to taste

freshly ground black pepper to taste

4 strips bacon, cooked but not crispy, chopped

2 cups loosely packed spinach leaves, chopped

1/3 cup chopped sundried tomatoes

1 cup chopped white button mushrooms (7 or 8 whole mushrooms)

butcher's twine

FOR SERVING DAY

5 cloves garlic, minced

2 Tbsp coconut oil

PREP DAY: Pound the flank steak with a meat mallet to an even ⅓-inch-thickness. Doing so will give you more surface area to work with when rolling the steak.

Lay the steak out flat, and season both sides with sea salt and pepper. Layer chopped bacon, spinach, sundried tomatoes, and mushrooms evenly over the steak.

Roll the steak tightly into a log (roulade), and tie it in 3 places with butcher's twine.

Wrap the steak in plastic wrap, seal it in a freezer bag, and freeze until needed.

SERVING DAY: Thaw the roulade in the refrigerator overnight.

When ready to cook, preheat your oven to 425°F.

In a large, oven-proof skillet over medium-high heat, melt the coconut oil.

Place the roulade in the skillet, and sear the steak until brown on all sides, 2-3 minutes total.

Remove the skillet from the heat, and sprinkle the minced garlic all over the roulade.

Place the skillet in the hot oven for 10-15 minutes or until the meat is cooked but still pink in the center.

Remove the skillet from the oven, and let the meat rest for 10 minutes.

Remove the twine, slice the roulade into pinwheels, and serve.

SERVES 4

Paleo Flatbread

1 cup tapioca flour/ tapioca starch

1/4 cup coconut flour, sifted

1/2 tsp garlic powder

1/2 tsp onion powder

1/4 tsp sea salt

1/2 cup canned coconut milk (full-fat)

1/4 cup coconut oil, melted

1 large egg, room temperature

2 tsp finely chopped, fresh rosemary

1/4 tsp cracked black pepper

Preheat the oven to 450°F. Cut a circle of parchment paper to fit in the bottom of a large cast-iron skillet. Place the parchment-lined skillet in the oven while it preheats.

In a large bowl, whisk together the tapioca flour, coconut flour, garlic powder, onion powder and salt.

In a separate bowl, whisk together the coconut milk, coconut oil and egg. Pour over the dry ingredients and stir to combine thoroughly. Set aside for 5 minutes.

Remove the hot skillet from the oven.

Transfer the batter into the skillet and carefully spread it out with a spatula to ¼- to ⅓-inch thickness. Sprinkle with the rosemary and pepper. Bake for 10–15 minutes, or until cooked throughout and lightly browned on the edges.

Cut flatbread into strips or wedges before serving. Can be served warm or at room temperature. (Store baked flatbread in an airtight container in the refrigerator for up to 3 days.)

Cain Credicott

SERVES 4

Salisbury Steak with Mushroom Gravy

FOR THE STEAKS

1 1/2 lb organic grass-fed ground beef

1/2 medium yellow onion, finely chopped

1 tsp granulated garlic

2 tsp granulated onion

1/2 tsp dried rosemary

1 tsp paprika

1 tsp fennel seed

1 tsp sea salt

freshly ground pepper to taste

2 Tbsp coconut oil, for the pan

FOR THE GRAVY

8 oz white mushrooms, chopped

sea salt and pepper to taste

2 cups organic beef broth

1/2 cup coconut milk (or your favorite nondairy milk)

1 Tbsp coconut flour

1 Tbsp arrowroot starch mixed with a tiny bit of cold water to make a slurry

Mix all of the steak ingredients gently in a bowl to combine.

Form 4 large oval patties, about 1" thick.

Heat oil in a large nonstick skillet over medium-high heat. Add steak patties to the hot pan.

Cook meat until browned and caramelized, about 6 minutes per side.

Remove patties to a platter and keep warm by tenting with foil.

Add mushrooms to hot pan. Season mushrooms with salt and pepper and cook until tender, about 5 minutes.

Add beef broth and coconut milk to pan.

Add coconut flour to pan and stir. Bring to a boil.

Add arrowroot slurry and stir until thick, about 1 minute. Remove gravy from heat.

Serve Salisbury steaks with mushroom gravy poured over the top!

Ben GREENFIELD + SONS

FOUNDER AND CEO OF KION

Ben Greenfield is a well known figure in the world of health and performance. He has a long history of high performance, from an accelerated education (graduated high school at 15 and started college at 16!) to training himself and guiding others.

Ben is dedicated to helping the world's hard-charging, high-achievers live a truly limitless life with fully optimized minds, bodies and spirits - all from his quiet home on 10 acres in the forested wilderness of Washington State. Ben combines intense time-in-the-trenches with ancestral wisdom and modern science to make your dreams a reality.

For the All Star Real Food Cookbook project, Ben wanted to contribute more than just recipes, he wanted to make sure to include his family. He asked his twin sons, River and Terran, to help him pick out their favorite recipes that a family can make together.

These recipes were written with those little helping hands in mind. Make sure to involve your family when you're preparing food!

You can find more on Ben at bengreenfieldfitness.com and learn about River and Terran at gogreenfields.com

www.bengreenfieldfitness.com

f /BGFitness   @bengreenfieldfitness

www.gogreenfields.com

f /gogreenfieldspodcast   @gogreenfieldsshow

RECIPES

Easy + Delicious Gluten-Free Fettuccine

Salmon Cakes

Chicken Salad Wraps

Handy Dandy Dandelion Snack

Pumpkin Custard

SERVES 4

Easy And Delicious Gluten-Free Fettuccine

PASTA

1 2/3 cup of gluten-free flour plus more for kneading and dusting

1 tsp of xanthan gum

3 medium eggs

2 Tbsp of water

PESTO

2 cups of fresh basil

1/2 cup of parmesan reggiano cheese

1/2 cup of olive oil

1/3 cup pine nuts

3 cloves of garlic

1/4 tsp of salt, more to taste

1/8 tsp of pepper, more to taste

In a bowl mix flour and xanthan gum until evenly distributed. Make a well in the middle of the dry ingredients. Add the eggs into the well. Now whisk the eggs and then slowly incorporate the dry ingredients.

If the dough is too dry, add cold water until dough holds together. Knead the dough for 2-3 minutes until smooth. Allow dough to rest for 15 minutes.

Use a pasta machine to flatten and cut the dough into a fettuccine cut.

Place the cut noodles onto a floured countertop and toss the noodles in the flour (this prevents them from sticking to one another).

Add the noodles into a pot of boiling water and cook for 3-4 minutes. Fresh pasta cooks much faster than dried pasta, test often!

Remove from boiling water and toss with pesto at your desired ratio of noodles to pesto.

PESTO: Pulse the basil and pine nuts in a food processor. Add in cheese and garlic, scrape the sides of the food processor, then slowly stream in oil and continue to blend. Stir in the salt and freshly ground pepper. Enjoy!

SERVES 2

Salmon Cakes

1/2 lb potatoes

3 x 6 oz cans of salmon, drained

2 Tbsp of Dijon mustard

1/4 cup of chopped chives

Salt and pepper to taste

4 eggs

1 cup coconut flakes

1 Tbsp oil, we use lard but you can use any cooking oil

AIOLI

3/4 cups of avocado mayo (we use Primal Kitchen Mayo)

1 lime juiced and zested

2 Tbsp of minced garlic

Salt and pepper to taste

Peel, chop, and boil the potatoes until you can easily slide a fork into them. While the potatoes are cooking, make the aioli.

Once potatoes are done cooking, strain and and mash.

Mix potatoes with salmon, Dijon mustard, chives, salt and pepper.

In a separate, shallow bowl, whisk the eggs.

Place the coconut flakes in a third, shallow bowl.

Once the salmon and potato batter is mixed together, form balls and flatten to ½ inch thick.

Drench the patties with the whisked eggs, then dip in coconut flakes to cover all sides.

Fry in lard until golden brown.

Place salmon cakes over a bed of sprouts and top with aioli. Enjoy!

AIOLI: Add avocado mayo, lime juice, lime zest, minced garlic, salt and pepper into a small bowl and stir until smooth.

SERVES 4

Chicken Salad Wraps

- 2-3 celery stalks
- 1 apple
- 3/4 cup walnuts
- salt and pepper
- 3/4 cups of avocado mayo (we like Primal Kitchen)
- 2 green onions
- 1 Tbsp of honey
- 2 Tbsp of apple cider vinegar
- 4 x 12 oz cans of chicken

String and cut your celery. Cut your apple into small cubes. Toast your walnuts and then chop. Mince the green onions.

Drain the juice from the chicken and crumble into a mixing bowl.

Add celery, walnuts, and onions. Stir until well mixed.

For the dressing, combine the honey, mayo, and vinegar. Mix until smooth and well blended.

Pour dressing over chicken salad and toss.

Wrap in tortilla or kale, and enjoy!

SERVES 2

Handy Dandy Dandelion Snack

3/4 cup gluten-free sourdough starter

1 cup washed dandelion flowers, pressed dry between paper towels

2 Tbsp grass fed butter

CUCUMBER LIME DIPPING SAUCE

1 brick of cream cheese

1 lime

1 red onion

1/2 cucumber (cut lengthwise)

2 cloves of garlic

SPICY MAYO DIPPING SAUCE

3 Tbsp of Sriracha

2 cups of mayo

Melt butter in a saucepan and heat 'til bubbling but not brown. Dip the dandelion heads into the sourdough starter, then fry in the saucepan, turning frequently.

CUCUMBER LIME DIPPING SAUCE: Soften the brick of cream cheese with the back of a spoon and cut into chunks that'll blend easily in a food processor.

Scrape the seeds out of your half cucumber with a spoon, then cut into sticks you can push into the processor.

Cut your peeled red onion into quarters and add to food processor.

Add the garlic, juice of the lime and the cheese, then pulse until finely chopped.

SPICY MAYO DIPPING SAUCE: Add the Sriracha and the mayo together and mix briefly.

Dip and enjoy!

SERVES 4

Pumpkin Custard

1 can pumpkin purée

1 cup cream

2 large eggs

1 tsp vanilla

1/4 cup honey

4 packs stevia

2 tsp pumpkin pie spice

1/2 tsp salt

COCONUT WHIPPED CREAM

1 can coconut milk

1 tsp honey

Preheat the oven to 350°F.

On a stovetop, combine pumpkin purée and cream into a sauce pan. Heat just until the cream boils.

In a medium bowl combine eggs, vanilla, honey, stevia, pumpkin spice, and salt.

Mix well, then pour the cream and pumpkin purée mixture into the egg mixture slowly while stirring the eggs quickly until all ingredients are combined into a smooth custard mixture.

Place ramekins into a 13"x 9" baking pan, then pour your custard mixture into individual ramekins.

Pour boiling water around the ramekins, fill the baking pan about an inch high.

Bake for 20-25 minutes or until they jiggle like jello.

Refrigerate for 2 hours and enjoy!

COCONUT WHIPPED CREAM: Blend coconut milk and honey in any blender, pour into a whipped cream dispenser. Add a dab of coconut whipped cream to each ramekin.

Dr. Terry WAHLS

PROFESSOR OF MEDICINE

Dr. Terry Wahls is a clinical professor of medicine at the University of Iowa. She is the author of The Wahls Protocol: How I Beat Progressive MS Using Paleo Principles and Functional Medicine, and the cookbook The Wahls Protocol Cooking for Life: The Revolutionary Modern Paleo Plan to Treat All Chronic Autoimmune Conditions. You can learn more about her work from her website, www.terrywahls.com. She hosts the Wahls Protocol Seminar every August where anyone can learn how to implement the Protocol with ease and success. Learn more about her MS clinical trials by reaching out to her team via this email: MSDietStudy@healthcare.uiowa.edu.

www.terrywahls.com

/TerryWahls

@drterrywahls

@terrywahls

RECIPES

Bacon Salad

Brats Skillet

Wahls Fudge

Slow Cooker Spaghetti Squash

Turkey Tacos

SERVES 1

Bacon Salad

An extremely hearty and filling warm salad with Brussels sprouts, beets, kale, and smoky, salty bacon! Look for nitrate-free bacon, preferably from a local processor. (This is easy to find in Iowa, where I live, but there are more and more brands producing high-quality nitrate-free bacon, so it is more widely available than ever before.)

BACON SALAD

1 bunch curly or lacinato kale

1 or 2 bacon slices

1/2 cup thinly sliced Brussels sprouts

1/2 cup grated or sliced raw carrots

2 Tbsp Balsamic Vinaigrette (see below)

1/4 cup grated raw beets

BALSAMIC VINAIGRETTE

6 Tbsp extra-virgin olive oil

2 Tbsp balsamic vinegar

1 tsp minced garlic

1/2 tsp sea salt

freshly ground black pepper

Cut the kale leaves from the thick stems and save the stems for another use. Roll up the leaves and thinly slice them crosswise. Steam them using a steamer basket and a sauce pan, or cook in a skillet with 1 tablespoon of water, and set them aside to cool. Alternatively, you can massage them with ¼ cup apple cider vinegar or lime juice and then let them sit for 30 minutes to an hour. (Both steaming and massaging with acid reduce the natural bitterness in kale.) This should yield approximately 3 cups of chopped kale leaves. Meanwhile, cook 1 or 2 slices of bacon on low for 10 to 12 minutes until desired level of crispness. Remove the bacon from the pan, and drain on paper towels. Add the Brussels sprouts and carrots to the bacon grease and cook for 3 to 5 minutes or until tender. Put the kale into a large bowl and drizzle with the dressing. Add the Brussels sprouts–carrot mixture and beets. Toss everything to coat. Crumble the bacon over the top of the salad.

VARIATION: For a meatier salad, you can add ½ cup cubed ham or Canadian bacon to the cooked vegetable mixture in the last minute of cooking, just to warm it up.

VARIATION FOR WAHLS DIET AND WAHLS PALEO: Add 2 tablespoons cooked or canned rinsed chickpeas to this salad.

BALSAMIC VINAIGRETTE: Put all the ingredients in a glass jar or bottle and shake to combine, or whisk all the ingredients together in a bowl until well combined. Shake or whisk again before each use. Store in the refrigerator for up to 5 days.

SERVES 4

Brats Skillet

4 bratwursts

1 cup sliced shiitake mushrooms

1/2 cup coarsely chopped onion

8 garlic cloves, minced

2 cups chopped red cabbage

4 cups chopped mustard greens

1/2 cup chopped fresh oregano

2 Tbsp ghee

Sriracha or spicy kimchi to taste

Boil the brats for 10 minutes, then slice them. Heat the ghee in a large skillet or stockpot over medium-high heat. Add the mushrooms, onion, and sliced brats and sauce until the mushrooms are soft and the onions are translucent, 2 to 5 minutes. Add garlic and cook, stirring for 2 minutes. Add the cabbage and cook for 5 minutes more. Remove from the heat and stir in the mustard greens and oregano. Cover and let skillet sit for 2 minutes.

Serve with Sriracha or spicy kimchi for an extra kick.

SERVES 20

Wahls Fudge

Wahls Fudge tastes like an indulgent, sweet treat but it's much more nutritionally dense than candy or other sweet desserts. In my house, Wahls Fudge makes any day feel like a holiday! Wahls Fudge is calorically dense, so it's excellent for those who are losing too much weight. If you are trying to lose weight, enjoy it sparingly.

1 cup coconut oil

1 medium avocado, pitted and peeled

1 cup raisins

1/2 cup dried unsweetened coconut

1 tsp unsweetened cocoa powder

Combine all the ingredients in a food processor. Process until smooth, then press the mixture into an 8"x 8" glass baking dish and refrigerate or place in a freezer for 30 minutes to firm up the fudge. Cut into 20 squares and enjoy. I usually store it in the refrigerator so it stays firm. The fudge keeps for about three days, but it rarely lasts that long.

MEXICAN CHOCOLATE VARIATION: Add 1 teaspoon ground cinnamon for a Mexican chocolate flavor.

WHITE CHOCOLATE VARIATION: The avocado is optional for the variation. Omit the cocoa powder. Add 1 teaspoon vanilla extract or ¼ teaspoon vanilla bean seeds. Swap raisins for golden raisins.

SERVES 4

Slow Cooker Spaghetti Squash

For grain-free eaters who miss pasta, one solution is spaghetti squash, a delicious and curiously pasta-like vegetable that you can top with all kinds of delicious sauces. Making it is simple if you use your slow cooker. The advantage to this is that you don't have to wrestle with trying to cut the squash in half. Just plop the whole thing in the slow cooker and set a timer. However, oven-roasting is also easy once you get the squash halved. You can roast or use your slow cooker to prepare all winter squash, such as butternut, acorn, and delicata.

1 medium spaghetti squash

1 Tbsp ghee, melted

1/4 cup nutritional yeast

sea salt and freshly ground black pepper

Put the spaghetti squash in the slow cooker, cover, and cook on low for 8 to 10 hours, or until the squash feels soft. Remove the squash and let it cool until you can handle it. Cut it in half lengthwise, scoop out the seeds, and scrape out the pasta-like strands with a fork.

Alternatively, preheat the oven to 375°F. Cut the squash in half lengthwise, scoop out the seeds, put the halves cut-side down in a large roasting pan or on a rimmed baking sheet, and roast for about 40 minutes, or until you can easily pierce the squash with a fork. Use a fork to scrape out the pastalike strands.

Put the spaghetti squash "noodles" in a large bowl and drizzle with ghee, then sprinkle with the nutritional yeast and sea salt and pepper to taste. You can also top this with your favorite bolognese or marinara sauce.

SERVES 4

Turkey Tacos

This recipe isn't a typical skillet recipe because instead of preparing your greens with the other ingredients in a stockpot or large skillet, you use the greens as a taco "shell". Butter lettuce and Boston lettuce or other greens, like mature curly kale or collard leaves, also work well

- 1 pound ground turkey
- 3 cups thinly sliced bell peppers
- 3 cups thinly sliced onions
- 3 garlic cloves, minced
- 8 large lettuce, kale, or collard leaves
- 2 Tbsp ghee
- 1/2 cup chopped fresh cilantro
- 1 Tbsp taco seasoning
- salsa and/or guacamole to taste
- favorite hot sauce to taste

Heat the ghee in a stockpot or large skillet over medium-high heat. Add the ground turkey, taco seasoning, bell peppers, onions, and garlic. Cook until turkey is browned and the vegetables are tender, 10 to 12 minutes.

Serve the cilantro and hot sauce on the side, or stir them directly into the skillet. Divide the taco filling among eight large leaf wrappers (lettuce, kale, or collards). Add salsa and/or guacamole. Roll up or fold up and enjoy. Alternatively, serve the filling on a bed of greens as a taco salad.

COOKING TIP: You don't need to add water or broth to the fat when you are cooking the meat for this meal.

Nicole DONATO

CONTRIBUTING WRITER FOR KETORESOURCE.ORG

Nicole Donato is a contributing writer for KetoResource.org. As a food enthusiast and writer, Nicole found the keto diet is medically proven with a history of success in a variety of medical settings. Nicole's search for a perfect diet developed into a passion for tailoring flavorful and nutritious recipes that follow the keto protocol.

www. ketoresource.org

RECIPES

Bacon Wrapped Asparagus + Eggs

Zoodles With Lemon, Basil + Shrimp

Brie Burger

Easy-Prep Keto Guacamole

Triple Berry Smoothie

SERVES 4

Bacon Wrapped Asparagus + Eggs

This treat is the perfect appetizer, mid-afternoon snack, or even fancy breakfast. I personally enjoy serving it to friends and family as the sunny side up eggs make the dish look impressive, while the bacon and asparagus are just plain delicious. Be sure to choose your bacon carefully, stay away from flavors of any kind (i.e. honey glazed). This dish makes keto seem easy!

8 free range grass-fed organic bacon slices

24 organic asparagus spears, divided

2 tsp minced organic garlic

1 tsp onion powder

1 tsp pink Himalayan sea salt, divided

1/2 tsp freshly ground black pepper, divided

2 Tbsp grass-fed free range organic butter

8 free range organic eggs

Preheat the oven to 400°F.

Wrap one bacon slice around each bundle of three asparagus spears. Place each bundle on a parchment lined baking sheet.

Sprinkle the garlic, onion powder, ½ teaspoon of salt, and a pinch of pepper over the bundles.

Place the tray in the preheated oven. Bake for 12 minutes, or until the bacon crisps.

In a large skillet over medium-high heat, melt the butter. Crack the eggs in pairs on the skillet. Try to keep the yolks intact.

Cook the eggs to your desired doneness, about 5 minutes for a runny egg. Season with the remaining ½ teaspoon of salt and the remaining pepper.

Remove the asparagus from the oven.

Remove the eggs from the skillet, placing two eggs atop two bundles of asparagus per serving.

SERVES 2

Zoodles With Lemon, Basil + Shrimp

This delicious dish is full of bright flavors. I personally like to buy my zoodles premade to cut down on the prep time. Be sure to use a high quality olive oil and fresh basil; Your taste buds will thank you! If you are running high on your protein macros this day, you can cut the shrimp portions to fit your macros. Finally, be prepared to serve this dish immediately. It's fantastic while still hot and fresh.

3 Tbsp organic extra-virgin olive oil

1/4 organic lemon, juiced

1 organic garlic clove, minced to paste

salt and pepper

1 ounce of organic, grass fed Parmesan cheese, grated (1/2 cup)

8 ounces wild caught extra-large shrimp (21 to 25 per pound) peeled, deveined, and tails removed

8 ounces zoodles (spiralized zucchini noodles)

2 Tbsp shredded fresh organic basil

1 Tbsp grass fed unsalted butter, softened

(optional) add tomatoes to taste (*Note: will change macros slightly)

Whisk the oil, lemon juice, garlic and ¼ teaspoon of salt together in a bowl, then stir in Parmesan cheese until thick and creamy.

Bring 4 quarts of water to a boil in a large pot. Add shrimp and 1 tablespoon of salt. Cook until shrimp is opaque throughout, about 1 minute. Using a slotted spoon, transfer the shrimp to a bowl. Season shrimp with salt and pepper to taste, then cover to keep warm.

Heat a skillet over medium heat. Add a pat of unsalted butter or olive oil. Toss in zoodles, and salt to taste. Sauté for several minutes, turning with tongs until the color of the zoodles deepen, and they become soft.

Once zoodles are prepared, add garlic/cheese mixture, butter, oil, and shrimp. Toss to combine. Top with basil, and season with salt and pepper to taste.

Serve immediately.

SERVES 4

Brie Burger

From time to time I really enjoy a delicious and well-made burger. The Brie cheese and Worcestershire sauce in this burger really ramp up the flavor to next level. In my keto world, this is a gourmet, yet casual dinner!

1 Tbsp grass-fed butter

1 large organic yellow onion, chopped

3 Tbsp Worcestershire sauce

1 small round organic, grass fed Brie, rind removed and cheese cut into 1/2 inch cubes

1 pound organic grass- fed ground beef

8 leaves of organic butter lettuce

Melt the butter over medium heat in a wide frying pan. Add the onion and stir to coat. Cook over fairly low heat, stirring occasionally, until the onion is very soft and a deep, sticky golden-brown. This will take approximately 20-30 minutes.

Mix Worcestershire sauce into the ground beef. Form two patties around the cubes of Brie. Season both sides lightly with salt and pepper.

Heat a flat pan over medium heat. Melt a pat of butter before adding the patties. Cook for approximately 4 to 8 minutes per side, based on your desired wellness. The USDA recommends that you cook your burger until the center is 160°F.

Before the burgers finish cooking, place the remaining Brie on top of your patties, and cover to help the cheese melt.

Once the cheese is melted and the burger has cooked, place the burger on two leaves of lettuce and place onions on burger. Enjoy!

Nicole Donato

SERVES 1

Easy-Prep Keto Guacamole

Sometimes I want something to snack on but I just don't have the time (or patience) to bake/cook/prepare something from scratch. This easy recipe goes from ingredients to reality in minutes!

1 oz pre-prepared pico de gallo

1 small organic avocado

salt and pepper

Halve avocado and remove the pit. Using a cross cut pattern, cut the avocado for easy removal. After cutting, use a spoon to remove the avocado from the skin.

Crush avocado, using a fork, until it has reached your desired creaminess.

Add the pico de gallo, and mix.

Salt and pepper to taste.

Enjoy!

SERVES 1

Triple Berry Smoothie

My biggest weakness is ice cream, which is why a smoothie is the perfect dessert for me. The iced treat is worth consuming a few less calories earlier in the day. The berries give me a sugary treat while the smoothie gives me the satisfaction of a milkshake! I recommend making only one serving per person, it helps keep from overindulging.

1 cup crushed ice

1/4 cup unsweetened almond milk

1/2 Tbsp coconut oil

1/4 cup blueberries

1/4 cup raspberries

1/4 cup blackberries

1/4 tsp pure vanilla extract

In a blender, place ½ cup of ice. Add the almond milk and coconut oil. Blend to combine.

Add the blueberries, raspberries, blackberries, vanilla, and the remaining ½ cup of ice. Blend until smooth, and serve.

Enjoy!

Erika PETERSON

CLEAN SIMPLE EATS FOUNDER

Erika is a wife and a mother of four. She is a certified health and wellness coach, recipe developer, food photographer and creator of Clean Simple Eats. Clean Simple Eats was born out of Erika's passion for healthy living and helping others after she had discovered the many amazing benefits from eating good quality food paired with an active lifestyle. She started sharing recipes online to teach people that eating healthy could be delicious, simple and fun. After 6 years of sharing recipes and quickly growing on her social media outlets, Erika's hobby has now turned into a rewarding career and business that she and her husband, JJ, run together full-time. Together they have helped thousands of people transform their health; physically, mentally and emotionally. Clean Simple Eats is a 7-week clean eating and exercise program designed to simplify healthy living for families and bring them back to the dinner table. Erika has rocked the typical dieting scene by putting a healthy spin on those delicious comfort food recipes we all know and love. Every recipe is balanced with the perfect amount of fat, carbs and protein to fuel your body, shed unwanted fat and provide sustainability for life. At the beginning of every season, Clean Simple Eats launches a 7-week challenge. They provide each participant with a seasonal meal plan, supplements and workouts to make the journey to better health a simple and fun experience. Each meal plan includes 90 macro-balanced and delicious recipes, a grocery list, menu planner and food prep guide for each week, HIIT workouts, gorgeous photos and one amazing community of like-minded people working toward becoming their best selves.

www.cleansimpleeats.com

RECIPES

Banana Nut Acai Bowl

Beef + Broccoli Stir-Fry

Chili-Lime Chicken Sliders

Mango Avocado Salsa

Sweet Cherry Almond Freeze

SERVES 1

Banana Nut Acai Bowl

1 frozen unsweetened Acai pack (I use Sambazon)

50g frozen strawberries

40g frozen bananas

1/4 cup unsweetened almond milk

1 serving protein powder

4-6 ice cubes

TOPPINGS

20g banana, sliced

1 Tbsp sliced almonds

1 Tbsp Paleo granola of your choice

Place frozen acai in a blender and pulse until broken up. Scrape down the sides of the blender and add the almond & coconut milk, frozen strawberries & bananas, protein powder and ice. Blend until smooth and thick.

Pour into a bowl and top with bananas, almonds and granola.

SERVES 4

Beef + Broccoli Stir-Fry

8 oz. sirloin tip steak

MARINADE

2 Tbsp coconut aminos or low sodium soy sauce

1 Tbsp honey

1/2 Tbsp olive oil

1 tsp rice vinegar

1/2 tsp minced garlic

VEGGIES

2 cups broccoli, chopped

1 cup sugar snap peas, chopped

1 cup water chestnuts

1 cup red onion, sliced

Whisk all marinade ingredients together.

Cut the steak into cubes and place in a Ziploc bag with marinade. Marinate 2+ hours in the fridge.

Heat a skillet to med/high heat. Spray the skillet with cooking spray and add steak. Discard the remaining marinade. Cook for two minutes per side. Remove from pan.

Spray the pan again and add veggies. Sauté for about five minutes or until veggies are tender. Add cooked steak back to the pan. Cook for one minute or until everything is heated through. Enjoy!

Erika Peterson

SERVES 4

Chili-Lime Chicken Sliders

16 oz. sweet potato

10 oz. chicken breast, raw

4 slices turkey bacon, halved

8 slices tomatoes

1 cup spinach leaves

1 avocado, mashed

CHILI-LIME MAYO

1/4 cup Paleo mayo of your choice

juice of 1/2 of a lime

1/4 tsp chili powder

dash onion powder

dash garlic powder

dash paprika

sea salt

ground black pepper

Heat oven to 400°F. Slice sweet potato into 16 equal rounds and place on a baking sheet lined with parchment paper. Spray tops with cooking spray and a sprinkle with salt. Bake for 35-40 minutes flipping halfway.

Butterfly cut your chicken. Heat a sauté pan over medium heat and grease with cooking spray. Cook chicken and bacon for five minutes per side or until golden and cooked through.

Make the Chili-Lime Mayo by beating all the ingredients together in a small bowl. Set aside.

Make sliders by layering half of the sweet potato rounds on the bottom then adding the mashed avocado, chicken, bacon, tomatoes & spinach. Spread the Chili-Lime Mayo evenly on the other sweet potato rounds and place on the top. Enjoy!

Erika Peterson

SERVES 4

Mango Avocado Salsa

- 1 mango, chopped
- 1 avocado, chopped
- 1/2 cup red bell pepper, chopped
- 1/4 cup red onion, chopped
- pinch cilantro, chopped
- juice from 1/2 a lime
- 1 Tbsp olive oil
- sea salt
- black pepper, ground

Place chopped mango, avocado, red bell peppers, red onions and cilantro in a food processer. Pulse until finely chopped. Pour into a bowl.

Add lime juice, olive oil and salt + pepper. Stir until well combined. Great paired with tacos, fish, pork loin or your favorite chips.

SERVES 1

Sweet Cherry Almond Freeze

1 cup unsweetened almond milk

1 cup frozen, pitted dark sweet cherries

1 serving vanilla protein powder

1 Tbsp natural almond butter

Stevia, optional

1/2 tsp almond extract

6-8 ice cubes

Place all ingredients in a high-powered blender. Blend on high until smooth.

Jenni HULET

AUTHOR MY PALEO PATISSERIE

Jenni Hulet is a photographer, blogger, and author of the best selling cookbook, My Paleo Patisserie. She runs the gluten-free lifestyle blog, The Urban Poser, and is a firm believer that food is always best when shared with others. Whether she's creating recipes, shooting photography, or teaching yoga, Jenni's greatest happiness is always found in helping others experience freedom and vibrancy in their lives, no matter what circumstances they may be facing. As a wife and mother of two growing teenage boys and one rambunctious rescue puppy, Jenni hasn't used the word 'leftovers' in at least 10 years.

www.theurbanposer.com

/theurbanposer

@theurbanposer

@theurbanposer

RECIPES

Vietnamese Style Chicken + Cabbage Salad

Pumpkin, Bacon + Chive Biscuits

Italian Almond Cookies

Maple Bacon Blondies

Chocolate Swirl Meringue

SERVES 1

Vietnamese Style Chicken + Cabbage Salad

SALAD

2 raw, boneless, skinless chicken breasts (about 10 ounces)

1 medium head, Savoy cabbage, thinly sliced or shredded (about 5 cups)

1 cup julienned carrots

4-5 scallions (spring onions), thinly sliced longways

1/4 cup mint leaves, roughly chopped

1/4 cup basil leaves, roughly chopped

1/4 cup cilantro leaves, roughly chopped

DRESSING

1/4 cup water

3 Tbsp fresh lime juice

2 Tbsp fish sauce

1/2 tsp apple cider vinegar

1 Tbsp olive oil

1/2 red seeded chili, chopped (optional)

Boil the chicken breasts in simmering water until cooked through to 160°F. Remove from the water and let them rest for 10 minutes. Once cool, thinly slice or shred with a fork and set aside.

Thinly slice or shred the cabbage, carrots, and spring onion tops (the green parts) into long strips, then roughly chop the herbs and place all the above ingredients into a large bowl and toss to combine well.

In a separate bowl, measure out all the dressing ingredients then mix 'til well combined.

Pour the dressing over the salad, toss and serve with Sriracha or other chili sauce. Adjust the salad to dressing ratios to suit your taste.

Jenni Hulet

SERVES 6 -7 COOKIES

Pumpkin, Bacon + Chive Biscuits

3-4 strips of bacon

1/2 cup melted fat, cooled (bacon fat, coconut oil or ghee)

1/2 cup coconut flour

3/4 tsp baking soda

1/4 tsp salt

1 Tbsp apple cider vinegar

1/2 cup pumpkin purée

1/4 cup shredded raw cheese

3 large eggs, room temp

1/4 cup finely chopped chives or green onions

Preheat oven to 350°F and line a large baking sheet with parchment paper.

Preheat a skillet over medium heat and cook the bacon until crispy. Remove bacon from the pan and leave to cool on a wire rack or paper towels. Once cool, break or cut into small pieces. Pour the bacon fat into a liquid measuring cup then add another fat of choice to make ½ cup total.

In a large bowl, whisk together the coconut flour, baking soda, and salt. Set aside.

In another bowl, whisk together the fat, vinegar, pumpkin purée, and eggs until well combined. Pour this liquid mixture into the flour mixture, and whisk till smooth. Fold the cheese, bacon, and chives into the batter until well combined.

Using a mechanical ice cream scoop (or ¼ cup measure) drop mounds of batter onto the prepared baking sheet, about 2 inches apart. Smooth the tops if needed.

Bake for 18-20 minutes, or until they're golden around the edges.

Allow the biscuits to cool for at least 5 minutes on the baking sheet before transferring them. The biscuits will be fragile while hot. Store in an airtight container for up to one day in the refrigerator.

SERVES 12 COOKIES

Italian Almond Cookies

2 cups almond flour

2/3 cup firmly packed maple sugar

2 large egg whites

pinch of salt

a few drops of almond extract

FOR THE COATING

1 large egg white

1/2 cup sliced almonds

Preheat the oven to 325°F. Line a cookie sheet with parchment paper.

Combine the flour and sugar in a large bowl. In a separate bowl, beat the two egg whites with a pinch of salt and a few drops of almond extract until they form soft peaks. Using a spatula, fold the beaten egg whites into the flour mixture, mixing until a smooth ball of dough has formed.

Make the coating: In a small bowl, beat the egg white with a fork for about 15 seconds. Place the sliced almonds on a small plate or in a shallow bowl. Set aside.

Divide the dough into 12 equal portions and shape them into small ovals, about 1½ inches long. You may need to wet and clean your hands periodically, as the dough will be slightly sticky.

Coat one cookie at a time on all sides with the beaten egg white, then roll or press in the sliced almonds. Arrange the cookies on the prepared cookie sheet, spacing them about 1 inch apart.

Bake for 25 to 30 minutes or until golden. Rotate the pan halfway through the baking time for even baking. Let cool on the pan.

These cookies are best eaten the day they are made but can be stored in an airtight container at room temperature for up to 3 days.

SERVES 16 BLONDIES

Maple Bacon Blondies

BLONDIES

1/2 cup palm shortening or ghee

2 1/4 cups almond flour

1 cup firmly packed maple sugar

1/4 tsp baking soda

1/4 tsp salt

2 large eggs

1 Tbsp vanilla extract

8 slices candied bacon

1/4 cup pecans, finely chopped

CANDIED BACON

3-4 pieces of bacon

about 1/3 cup maple syrup

FOR THE CANDIED BACON: Make the candied bacon before starting the brownies as it will need to cool down before breaking it up into tiny pieces for the topping.

Preheat the oven to 375°F

On a parchment paper lined rimmed cookie sheet, lay out the strips of bacon. You want the rim so that your bacon grease doesn't run down into oven and start a grease fire. (Not that I would know anything about that)

Using a pastry brush, sweep a generous amount of maple syrup over each piece of bacon. You could also sprinkle maple sugar instead of using syrup, but I find that it takes less syrup and it goes on smoother and faster.

Bake in the preheated oven for about 10 minutes. Remove the baking sheet from oven and flip the bacon over. Brush the other side with maple syrup and return to the oven for another 8-10 minutes or until dark and caramel-y. Watch the bacon closely toward the end, it burns fast. Times will vary from oven-to-oven (most basic ovens don't actually read temps accurately). For best results use an oven thermometer.

Remove from oven and cool. I like to place my bacon on a plate and chill in the freezer. This both speeds up the cooling process and makes them easier to cut in to small pieces.

Cut or break the bacon into small pieces.

FOR THE BLONDIES: Grease an 8-inch square cake/brownie pan and line it with parchment paper. Leave flaps on two sides of the pan for easy removal of the blondies.

In a small saucepan over medium heat, melt the shortening just until it becomes liquid. Set aside to cool.

In a large bowl, whisk together the flour, sugar, baking soda, and salt until blended. In a separate bowl, lightly beat the eggs, vanilla, and melted shortening, then add the egg mixture to the flour mixture and stir until the batter is well combined and there are no lumps.

Transfer the batter to the prepared pan. It will be quite thick, so smooth it out as best you can.

Break the candied bacon into small pieces, then sprinkle the top of the batter evenly with the candied bacon and pecan pieces.

Bake for 22 to 25 minutes or until the blondies are golden and the center springs back when gently pressed. Remove from the oven and let cool in the pan for at least 10 minutes.

Run a knife along the outside edge of the blondies, pull up on the paper flaps, and remove from the pan. Cut into squares and serve. The blondies can also be cut in the pan. They store well, covered, at room temperature for about 2 days. They're also delicious chilled.

SERVES 6 MERINGUES

Chocolate Swirl Meringue

3 large egg whites, room temperature

3/4 cup firmly packed maple sugar

1 tsp vanilla extract

1/4 tsp apple cider vinegar

8 ounces bittersweet chocolate, melted and cooled

Preheat the oven to 250°F. Line a cookie sheet with parchment paper.

Place the egg whites in the bowl of a stand mixer fitted with a whisk attachment. Beat on medium speed until soft peaks form. Sprinkle in the sugar, then add the vanilla and vinegar. Increase the mixer speed to high and beat until the sugar has completely dissolved and the meringue holds stiff glossy peaks.

Drizzle some of the cooled chocolate over the meringue, but do not stir it in. The swirl will be mostly on the outside, though some will sink into the cookies. Scoop out 6 large spoonfuls of the meringue, drizzling on more chocolate before scooping each one, and drop them onto the lined cookie sheet, spacing them about 2 inches apart.

Bake the meringues for 40 to 50 minutes or until they easily peel off of the parchment paper. Turn off the oven, crack open the oven door, and let the meringues cool in the oven for about 1 hour.

These cookies are best eaten the day they are made but can be stored in an airtight container in the fridge for a few days.

JJ VIRGIN

CELEBRITY NUTRITION EXPERT

Celebrity nutrition expert and Fitness Hall of Famer JJ Virgin teaches clients how to break through food and carb intolerances, so they can finally lose the weight to transform their health and their lives.

JJ is a prominent TV and media personality, whose previous features include co-host of *TLC's Freaky Eaters*, health expert for *Dr. Phil*, and appearances on *PBS*, *Dr. Oz*, *Rachael Ray*, *Access Hollywood*, and the *TODAY* Show. She also speaks regularly and has shared the stage with notables including TD Jakes, Tony Robbins, and Brendon Burchard. JJ is the author of four NY Times bestsellers: *The Virgin Diet*, *The Virgin Diet Cookbook*, *JJ Virgin's Sugar Impact Diet*, and *JJ Virgin's Sugar Impact Diet Cookbook*.

Her latest book, *Warrior Mom: 7 Secrets to Bold, Brave Resilience,* shows mothers everywhere how to be strong, positive leaders for their families while exploring the inspirational lessons JJ learned as she fought for her own son's life. JJ hosts the popular JJ Virgin Lifestyle Show podcast, with 4 million downloads and counting. She also regularly writes for Rodale Wellness, Mind Body Green, and other major blogs and magazines.

www.jjvirgin.com

f / JJVirginOfficial

@jj.virgin

@jjvirgin

RECIPES

Vanilla Almond Paleo Protein Pancakes

Perfect Paleo Smoothie

Paleo Egg Roll Bowl

Paleo Steamed Broccoli with Garlic Oil Drizzle

Paleo Pumpkin Brownies

SERVES 2

Vanilla Almond Paleo Protein Pancakes

1 cup blanched almond flour (superfine ground almonds)

1 tsp baking soda

1/2 tsp JJ Virgin Sprinkles or other low-sugar impact sweetener

pinch sea salt

2 eggs

1/4 cup water

2 tsp vanilla extract

1/4 tsp almond extract

coconut oil for pan

Whisk almond flour, baking soda, JJ Virgin Sprinkles, and the pinch of sea salt together in a medium mixing bowl until there're no lumps.

In a small mixing bowl, whisk together the eggs, water, and vanilla and almond extracts. Add the liquid ingredients to the dry ingredients and whisk together until thoroughly mixed.

Preheat a lightly oiled nonstick pan over medium-low heat.

Drop batter by 2 tablespoonfuls onto the prepared pan, and cook until pancakes are golden brown and edges are dry, about 3-4 minutes.

Flip and cook until browned on the other side, 2-3 minutes. Repeat with remaining batter.

Serve your pancakes with full-fat nut milk yogurt, fresh berries, and a sprinkle of cacao nibs or sliced almonds.

JJ Virgin

SERVES 1

Perfect Paleo Smoothie

2 scoops JJ Virgin Paleo-Inspired All-In-One Protein Shake powder (your choice of chocolate or vanilla)

10 oz. unsweetened almond milk

1 cup frozen organic strawberries or blueberries

1 cup fresh or frozen spinach

2 Tbsp sunflower seed butter

1 Tbsp chia seeds

Blend the ingredients together until smooth.

Your smoothie can be thickened by adding ice cubes or thinned by adding more almond milk or cold water.

SERVES 4

Paleo Egg Roll Bowl

- 1 lb organic free range chicken breast or pastured pork loin, cut into bite-size cubes
- 3 Tbsp coconut aminos, divided
- 2 Tbsp coconut oil, divided
- 2 tsp grated fresh ginger
- 3 cloves garlic, minced
- 3 scallions, thinly sliced and divided into green and white
- 8 oz. coleslaw mix with shredded cabbage and carrot
- 4 oz. organic mushrooms, thinly sliced both lengthwise and crosswise to create rectangles
- 1 organic zucchini, cut into thin 2"-long rectangles
- 1 Tbsp sesame oil
- 1 Tbsp rice vinegar
- 1 Tbsp sesame seeds, plus more for sprinkling (white or black)
- 1/2 tsp ground black pepper
- dash crushed red pepper flakes (optional)

Heat 1 tablespoon of coconut oil in large skillet over medium-high heat.

Add chicken or pork cubes, 1 tablespoon of coconut aminos, the grated ginger, garlic, and the white parts of the sliced scallions.

Cook while stirring until meat is cooked through and lightly browned, 7-9 minutes.

Add remaining tablespoon of coconut oil, remaining 2 tablespoons aminos, and the rest of the ingredients. Cook and stir over medium heat until veggies are tender, 10-15 minutes.

Taste for seasoning, then top with a final sprinkle of sesame seeds.

SERVES 4

Paleo Steamed Broccoli with Garlic Oil Drizzle

8 cups broccoli florets

2 Tbsp extra-virgin olive oil

5 clove garlic, thinly sliced

1/8 tsp red pepper flakes

1 Tbsp grated lemon zest

1/4 tsp sea salt

Bring a large pot of lightly salted water to a boil over high heat.

Add the broccoli to the pot and return to a boil, then cook for 6-8 minutes. Drain in a colander, then transfer to a large bowl and set aside.

Heat the oil in a large nonstick skillet over medium. Add the garlic and red pepper flakes and cook until the garlic just starts to brown around the edges, 2 to 3 minutes.

Pour the mixture over the broccoli and stir in the lemon zest and salt; toss well. Serve warm or at room temperature.

SERVES 8

Paleo Pumpkin Brownies

1 cup canned pumpkin puree (NOT pumpkin pie filling)

1/2 cup unsweetened salted almond butter (if not salted, add a pinch of sea salt to recipe)

5 Tbsp raw cacao powder

1 tsp JJ Virgin Sprinkles or powdered monk fruit (or to taste)

oil for pan

Preheat oven to 350°F.

Generously oil an 8"x 4" loaf pan with coconut oil or avocado oil.

Beat together the ingredients in a mixing bowl using an electric mixer. Transfer batter to greased loaf pan and smooth into even layer.

Bake at 350°F for 40-45 minutes, until a wooden skewer inserted in the center comes out mostly clean.

Cool in the pan completely before cutting into 8 brownies. (You can put the pan in the refrigerator to speed that process up.)

Store leftover brownies in airtight container in refrigerator for up to 5 days. Brownies also freeze beautifully for up to 6 weeks!

Dr. Kellyann PETRUCCI

BESTSELLING AUTHOR

Kellyann Petrucci, M.S., N.D., is the author of the New York Times bestselling book Dr. Kellyann's Bone Broth Diet, Dr. Kellyann's Bone Broth Cookbook, and The 10-Day Belly Slimdown. She also is the host of the PBS specials, 21 Days to a Slimmer, Younger You and The 10-Day Belly Slimdown and transformations are her passion. As a weight loss and natural anti-aging specialist she has personally helped hundreds of people go from overweight and sick to youthful and healthy. Through her books, ecourses, webinars, and appearances she has been able to help thousands more. Dr. Petrucci did postgraduate work in Europe, studying naturopathic medicine in England and Switzerland. She is one of the few practitioners in the United States certified in biological medicine by the esteemed Dr. Thomas Rau of the Paracelsus Klinik Lustmühle in Switzerland. Dr. Petrucci is also the driving force behind the popular website drkellyann.com, a weekly contributor on Dr. Oz and appears regularly on Good Morning America and other national news programs. She has authored six best-selling books for John Wiley & Sons. In addition, she is a regular contributor to the Huffington Post and MindBodyGreen. She has been featured in the Wall Street Journal, Woman's World, Life & Style, Closer, Harper's Bazaar, Daily Mail, Cooking Light, Redbook, and more.

Currently, Dr. Petrucci is focusing much of her attention on developing innovative beauty and food-based products.

www.drkellyann.com

/drkellyann

@drkellyannpetrucci

RECIPES

Bloody Mary with Bacon

Braised Brussel Sprouts with Bacon

Coconut Cake

Korean Rice Bowl

Turkey Kale Meatballs with Zucchini Noodles and Salsa Cruda

SERVES 2

Bloody Mary with Bacon

1 cup homemade beef broth, Dr. Kellyann's Broth in beef or Dr. Kellyann's Collagen Broth

1 cup organic tomato or vegetable juice

1 Tbsp freshly squeezed lime juice

1/2 tsp Worcestershire sauce

1/2 tsp tabasco or your favorite hot sauce

1/4 tsp prepared horseradish, or more to taste

dash freshly ground pepper

dash Celtic or pink Himalayan salt if juice is salt-free

2 ounces potato vodka

ice cubes

GARNISH OPTIONS

cooked bacon strips, celery stalks, cooked shrimp, Spanish olives, or lime wedges

Combine all ingredients in a pitcher or drink shaker. Pour into two tall glasses. Add additional ice if desired and garnish with your choice of garnishes.

VARIATION: Bloody Maria: Substitute Padron tequila for vodka and add ¼ to ½ teaspoon sauce from canned chipotle in adobo. This imparts a smoky, hotter taste to the cocktail.

SERVES 4

Braised Brussels Sprouts with Bacon

4 slices uncured bacon

1 pound medium brussels sprouts, trimmed and halved

1 large shallot, thinly sliced

1/4 tsp Celtic or Himalayan sea salt

1/4 tsp freshly ground black pepper

1/3 cup chicken bone broth

2 tsp Dijon mustard

1 1/2 tsp chopped fresh thyme

In a large skillet, cook the bacon over medium heat until crisp, about 8 minutes. Remove the bacon to a plate lined with paper towels. Crumble when cool.

Add the brussels sprouts to the skillet, cut side down. Cook, undisturbed, until the sprouts start to take color, about 2 minutes. Add the shallot, tossing to combine, and cook until the shallot begins to soften, about 2 minutes. Sprinkle with salt and pepper. Add ¼ cup of of the broth to the skillet, cover, and cook until the sprouts are crisp tender, about 3 minutes more.

In a small bowl, combine the mustard, thyme and remaining broth. Stir the sauce into the sprouts. Cook, stirring, until well combined, about 1 minute. Serve the sprouts topped with the crumbled bacon.

SERVES 12

Coconut Cake

FOR THE CAKE

1 cup coconut flour

1/2 tsp salt

1/2 tsp baking soda

8 large eggs

1/2 cup coconut oil, melted

1/2 cup maple syrup

2 tsp vanilla extract

FOR THE FROSTING

1/2 cup unsweetened cocoa powder

1/4 cup coconut oil, melted

2 Tbsp maple syrup

1/4 tsp vanilla extract

pinch of salt

For the cake: Preheat the oven to 350°F. Coat an 8 inch round cake pan with coconut oil spray and line the bottom with a round of parchment paper.

In a medium bowl, stir together the coconut flour, salt, and baking soda. In a stand mixer fitted with the paddle attachment, mix the eggs, coconut oil, maple syrup, and vanilla until well combined. Add the dry ingredients and mix well, making sure there are no lumps.

Spread the batter into the prepared pan and bake until golden and brown around the edges, 25 to 30 minutes. Let cool in the pan for 10 minutes, then turn onto a rack to cool completely.

For the frosting: In a bowl, stir together the cocoa, coconut oil, maple syrup, vanilla, and salt until smooth. Spread on the cooled cake.

SERVES 4

Korean Rice Bowl

2 Tbsp coconut aminos

1 tsp toasted sesame oil

1 tsp grated fresh ginger

1 clove garlic, minced

1 pound beef sirloin, trimmed

1 cup brown rice (or use cauliflower rice)

3 medium carrots, thinly sliced

4 ounces shiitake mushrooms, stems discarded, caps sliced

5 ounces baby spinach

2 tsp olive oil

4 large eggs

1 cup kimchi

hot pepper sauce of choice (optional)

In a large bowl, stir together the coconut aminos, sesame oil, ginger and garlic. Add the beef and set aside to marinate while you cook rice and vegetables.

Cook the rice according to pack directions. Set aside and keep warm. If using cauliflower rice, saute until warm.

In a medium pot fitted with a steamer basket, bring 1 inch of water to a boil. Steam the vegetables separately in the basket; carrots until crisp tender, shiitakes until softened and spinach until wilted and bright green, about 2 minutes each. Set each aside and keep warm.

In a large skillet, heat 1 teaspoon of olive oil over medium heat until simmering. Remove the steak from the marinade (discard the marinade) and cook, turning halfway through until a thermometer inserted in the center registers 160° for medium, 8 minutes (or until desired doneness). Rest the steak for 10 minutes before slicing very thinly.

Wipe out the skillet, heat the remaining 1 teaspoon of olive oil and cook the eggs sunny side up, about 2 minutes.

To serve, divide the rice among 4 bowls. Top each with steamed vegetables, kimchi, beef, and 1 egg. Serve with hot pepper sauce on the side, if desired.

SERVES 4

Turkey Kale Meatballs with Zucchini Noodles and Salsa Cruda

FOR THE MEATBALLS

1 pound ground turkey

10 ounces frozen kale, thawed

1/2 cup minced yellow onion

1/2 cup grated carrot

2 large egg whites

1 clove garlic, minced

Celtic or Himalayan sea salt

FOR THE SALSA CRUDA AND NOODLES

2 tomatoes, coarsely chopped

1/2 medium yellow onion, chopped

1 clove garlic, minced

2 Tbsp olive oil

1 Tbsp balsamic vinegar

3 medium zucchini, spiralized or peeled

2 tablespoons thinly sliced basil leaves

For the meatballs: Position a rack in the center of the oven and preheat to 425°F. Line a large rimmed baking sheet with foil or parchment paper and coat with coconut oil spray.

In a large bowl, combine all of the ingredients and a pinch of salt and pepper. Wet hands, form 12 meatballs the size of golf balls. Place on the prepared baking sheet and coat with more coconut oil spray. Bake until no longer pink and lightly golden, turning the meatballs halfway through, about 18 minutes.

Meanwhile, for the salsa and noodles: In a medium bowl, toss together the tomatoes, onion, garlic, oil, and vinegar. Season to taste with salt and pepper.

Divide the zucchini noodles among 4 plates. Top with the salsa, 3 meatballs each and a sprinkle of fresh basil.

Leanne ELY

SAVINGDINNER.COM FOUNDER

SavingDinner.com is the original menu planning website! Leanne Ely began creating Menu-Mailer on SavingDinner.com in 2001 to help families get back to the dinner table. Within just a few years, Readers Digest declared a new industry had been born - the menu planning industry - and Leanne was dubbed the "mother" of menu planning.

SavingDinner.com's goal is to bring families closer together by enjoying healthy and easy-to-prepare meals.We do this by creating innovative menu planning products like Premium Menu-Mailer, which includes delicious and nutritious recipes, shopping lists and nutritional information!

SavingDinner.com also features an informative daily blog where you can find nutritional tips and tricks, delicious recipes and the tools you need to eat healthy and prepare delicious family dinners!

What can we help you find?

www.savingdinner.com

f /SavingDinner

@savingdinner

RECIPES

Garlic Lime Chicken

Roasted Brussels Sprouts with Bacon + Shallots

Stone Fruit with Almond Hazelnut Chia Seed Brittle + Vanilla Bean Coconut Cream

The Easiest + Best Guacamole

Raspberry Lemon Frosé

SERVES 4

Garlic Lime Chicken

1/2 tsp salt

1/2 tsp pepper

1/8 tsp cayenne pepper

1/8 tsp paprika

1 tsp garlic powder

1/2 tsp onion powder

1/2 tsp thyme

4 boneless skinless chicken breast halves

1 1/2 Tbsp butter

1 1/2 Tbsp olive oil

3 Tbsp lime juice

1/3 cup low sodium chicken broth

small handful cilantro, chopped (optional)

In a small bowl, combine first 7 ingredients; sprinkle mixture on both sides of chicken breast halves.

In a skillet, heat butter and olive oil together over medium-high heat; saute chicken until golden brown, about 5 minutes on each side; remove from skillet and keep warm.

Add lime juice and chicken broth to the skillet, whisking up all of the browned bits from the bottom of the pan. Cook until sauce has reduced slightly.

Return chicken to the skillet to thoroughly coat with the sauce; garnish with cilantro and serve.

SERVES 4

Roasted Brussels Sprouts with Bacon + Shallots

1 1/2 pounds brussels sprouts, outer leaves removed, halved

2 medium shallots, cut into thin wedges

4 slices of bacon, partially cooked and chopped

1 Tbsp bacon fat (reserved from cooking bacon)

1 1/2 Tbsp ghee

sea salt and fresh ground pepper

Preheat oven to 400°F.

In a cast iron skillet or other ovenproof pan, toss together all ingredients (brussels through salt and pepper).

Once fully combined, place into preheated oven. Roast for 20 to 30 minutes, or until top leaves are slightly charred and brussels are fork tender.

Serve warm.

SERVES 4

Stone Fruit with Almond Hazelnut Chia Seed Brittle + Vanilla Bean Coconut Cream

- 2 Tbsp chia seeds
- 1/2 cup chopped OR slivered almonds
- 1/2 cup chopped hazelnuts
- 1/2 cup grass fed unsalted butter (1 stick)
- 1 cup pure maple syrup
- 1 1/2 Tbsp coconut sugar
- 1 tsp vanilla extract
- 1 tsp baking soda
- 1 (14 ounce) can full fat coconut milk
- 1 vanilla bean, scraped (OR 1/2 teaspoon vanilla bean paste)
- 1 pound stone fruit of choice (we used peaches and nectarines - though it's also excellent with cherries, plums, apricots, pluots, etc)

Line a small baking sheet with parchment paper, and evenly scatter the chia seeds, almonds, and hazelnuts. Keep them relatively close together so there isn't a lot of negative space in between.

In a medium sauce pan, over medium heat, add butter. Once melted, add in maple syrup and coconut sugar. Whisk together well.

Using a candy thermometer**, bring mixture to about 300°F, then remove from heat and quickly whisk in vanilla extract and baking soda. Once thoroughly combined, immediately pour mixture over the scattered chia seeds and nuts, using a spatula to evenly cover all of them.

Place in freezer for about 45 minutes or until it sets and hardens.

While waiting on the brittle to set, prepare the coconut cream.

In a small pot, over medium low heat, add full fat coconut milk. If the water and coconut fat have separated, DO NOT add the water! Just get the creamy good stuff! Once it thins slightly over the heat, add in the vanilla bean. Whisk together and remove from heat (DO NOT LET IT BOIL, only heating it enough to make the cream more pliable).

Then slice the stone fruit and distribute them to small bowls or plates. Pour coconut cream over the top of the fruit, and top with a couple pieces of the finished brittle. Enjoy!

**If you don't have a candy thermometer, keep the mixture boiling over medium heat for about 3 to 5 minutes, until it starts smelling slightly of burnt sugar and becomes really really thick.

SERVES 4 - 6

The Easiest + Best Guacamole

4 large Hass avocados, pitted and cubed

1/2 a small red onion, diced fine

1 large lime, juiced

1/3 cup chopped cilantro

3 Tbsp pico de gallo, OR your favorite salsa

sea salt, to taste

In a large bowl, mash all ingredients together - we like it chunky, but feel free to mash until you get your preferred texture!

Serve with just about anything!

Yep, it's that easy! Everyone will rave about how delicious it is, guaranteed!

SERVES 4

Raspberry Lemon Frosé

1 bottle of rosé

1 medium lemon, juiced

1 cup frozen raspberries (golden or regular)

1/3 cup vodka

Prepare ahead: fill an ice cube tray with the rosé (there will still be most of the bottle left over), and place in freezer.

Once rosé is frozen, place rosé ice cubes into a blender, along with the lemon juice, frozen raspberries, vodka, and a cup of the remaining rosé.

Blend until smooth, and then strain with a mesh strainer to remove the seeds from the raspberries.

Pour into a glass and enjoy! And if it melts too much, just throw the blended frosé back in the freezer until it's firmed up a bit more!

Mark SISSON

BESTSELLING AUTHOR

Mark Sisson is founder of Primal Nutrition, LLC, and Primal Kitchen, LLC, and the publisher of MarksDailyApple.com, the #1-ranked blog for over a decade in its health and fitness category. Mark unveiled his groundbreaking book, *The Keto Reset Diet*, in 2017, making the New York Times bestseller list. He's the author of numerous books, including *The Primal Blueprint*, which was credited with turbocharging the growth of the primal/paleo movement back in 2009.

www.primalkitchen.com

f /marksdailyapple

@primalkitchenfoods

RECIPES

Low-Carb Chocolate Mug Cake

Bacon Pancakes

Slow Cooker Pork-Stuffed Peppers

Primal Egg Yolk Coffee

Mexican Grilled Corn with Classic Mayo + Cotija

SERVES 1

Low-Carb Chocolate Mug Cake

- 1 Tbsp unsalted butter
- 2 Tbsp super fine almond flour
- 1 Tbsp raw cacao powder
- 1/2 tsp baking powder
- pinch of salt
- 1 Tbsp heavy cream
- 1/4 tsp vanilla extract
- 8 drops liquid stevia (add more or less, depending on your preference)
- 1 large egg yolk
- 9 grams (3 squares) dark chocolate (85% cacao), chopped

Melt the butter into a small mug, in the microwave (about 20 seconds).

Mix in the almond flour, cacao powder, baking powder and a tiny pinch of salt until thick and smooth.

Add the heavy cream, vanilla extract, and liquid stevia. Mix until smooth, then add the egg yolk and mix again until smooth.

Stir in the dark chocolate.

Put the mug back in the microwave and cook for 50 seconds. Microwaves vary, so the exact cooking time can vary as well, but overcooking the mug cake will make it dry and burn the bits of dark chocolate. Err on the side of undercooking, rather than overcooking the cake.

This low-carb mug cake has the best texture and flavor when it's freshly baked and warm, so enjoy immediately!

SERVES 2

Bacon Pancakes

- 6 slices of bacon
- 3 egg whites*
- 1/4 cup coconut flour
- 1 Tbsp purified granular gelatin
- 2 Tbsp unsalted butter, melted
- 2 Tbsp finely chopped chives
- 1/2 cup water

Cook the bacon in a frying pan over medium heat. Leave the bacon fat in the pan. Crumble or finely chop the bacon and set aside.

Whisk egg whites into soft peaks (an electric mixer works well for this). Set aside.

In a large bowl mix together the coconut flour, gelatin, butter, chives and bacon. Add the water and mix well then gently fold in the egg whites until combined. The batter will be thick and lumpy.

Re-heat the bacon fat in the frying pan over medium heat. Scoop small amounts (about 2 tablespoons) of batter into the pan, gently smoothing the batter out with a spoon to form small pancakes.

Better yet, set a 3-inch biscuit cutter in the frying pan, drop the batter in the middle and then smooth out the batter to form perfectly round cakes.

Cook about 3 minutes on each side. Serve warm.

*Using the entire egg instead of just the whites can be done but it makes a heavier, less fluffy pancake.

Top with full-fat sour cream and diced chives, if desired.

SERVES 2-4

Slow Cooker Pork-Stuffed Peppers

2 pounds ground pork (or a combination of pork and beef)

4-8 large bell peppers*

1 large onion

2 carrots

4 cloves of garlic

1/2 head of cauliflower

6 ounce can of tomato paste*

*can sub: 1/4 cup Primal Kitchen ketchup for tomato paste

1 Tbsp dry oregano

1 Tbsp dry or fresh tarragon

1 1/2 - 2 tsp salt

1 - 1 1/2 tsp fresh ground pepper

Cut the tops of the peppers and clean the seeds out.

Arrange peppers in an Instant Pot or slow cooker standing up and make sure they fit securely.

Grate onion, carrots, garlic and cauliflower in the food processor. You can also just chop them into small pieces with a knife if you don't have a food processor.

In a big bowl, combine ground pork, shredded vegetables, seasonings and tomato paste. Add salt and pepper. Stuff the peppers with the mixture and arrange leftover meat between the peppers. Add half a cup of water, cover and cook on low for 8-10 hours. If using an Instant Pot, use the Slow Cooker Medium Setting with non-pressurized lid and cook for 8-10 hours.

*Recipe makes enough filling for 8 bell peppers.

SERVES 1

Primal Egg Yolk Coffee

1 1/2 cup coffee

3 pastured egg yolks

1 tsp sugar

1/4 tsp of salt

First, I brew the coffee (35 grams of coffee beans – I use a light roast, single-origin bean) in a French press. Dump the grinds in, add about 350 ml of water, give it a quick stir, cover it, and let it sit for three minutes. Meanwhile, I separate the yolks from the whites. Once the coffee is ready, I dump it in a blender, set it to "low," and drop in the yolks. After a few seconds, I add a teaspoon of sugar and a pinch of salt (around a quarter teaspoon) and let it blend a bit more. I pour it, admire the head of foam, and get to drinking.

SERVES 8

Mexican Grilled Corn with Classic Mayo + Cotija

Primal Kitchen Avocado Oil Spray

1 tsp chile powder

1/2 tsp cayenne powder

8 ears of corn, husked

1/4 cup Primal Kitchen Mayo with Avocado Oil

1/2 cup cotija cheese

1 lime

Build medium-sized fire in a charcoal grill, or heat your gas grill to high. Spray your grill grate with Primal Kitchen Avocado Oil Spray.

Combine chile powder and cayenne in a small bowl.

Gently add the corn to the grill, turning them occasionally. Grill the corn until they're cooked through and slightly charred, about 10 minutes.

Remove the corn cobs from the grill, and immediately brush each ear with 2 tsp of Primal Kitchen Classic Mayo.

Top each cob with a sprinkle of cotija cheese and a pinch of the chile powder mixture.

Squeeze 1 lime over each ear of corn, and serve.

Enjoy!

Nik HAWKS and Lee SELMAN

PALEO TREATS® CO-FOUNDERS

Nik Hawks and Lee Selman have been running Paleo Treats since inception in 2009. Seeing that Paleo (at the time) had basically no dessert options other than fruit, they started making Paleo Treats in their kitchen, took it up to the '09 CrossFit Games and saw immediate success and traction.

From there, they built a business that has since been recognized by FedEx (Top Ten Small Businesses in America), Paleo Magazine (Best Guilt Free Dessert) and received critical acclaim in the Paleo and real food community.

With backgrounds from camel handling to military service and a wealth of odd jobs, they bring a wide spectrum of experience and knowledge to the business of Paleo Treats. Of course, a dessert company needs to focus on dessert, and boy do Nik & Lee enjoy a sweet treat.

They LOVE to be in the kitchen; Lee does the cooking and Nik does the dishes. Lee is the creator of the majority of Paleo Treats recipes and is especially proud of her favorite, the Cacao Now.

Their daily ritual of a butter coffee in the morning is included in the recipe section of this book. Give it a whirl and see how well it works for you.

Based out of San Diego, their interests range from evolutionary lifestyle to Phillipino knife fighting and from paragliding to gardening. You can usually find them in the Paleo Treats shop during at least some part of every day. Come visit!

www.paleotreats.com

f /paleotreatsfan

@paleotreats

@paleotreats

RECIPES

Avocado Chocolate Mousse

Banana Pancakes

Nik's Butter Coffee

Paleo Pizza Crust

Seed & Nut Paleo Bread

SERVES 2

Avocado Chocolate Mousse

This Paleo avocado mousse recipe is for those days when you're willing to wait for dessert if you have to but you sure wouldn't mind licking the bowl clean while the dessert cools in the fridge.

- 2 large ripe avocados
- 2 Tbsp honey
- 4 Tbsp high quality cocoa powder
- 1 tsp cinnamon
- 2-4 Tbsp alternative milk of your choice

FOR THE COCONUT WHIPPED CREAM

- 1 can of full fat coconut milk
- 1 tsp vanilla (optional)
- 1 tsp honey (optional)

Cut your avocados in half and carefully remove the pit. Scoop out the avocado flesh with a spoon. Pop the avocado halves into a high powered blender or food processor. Add the honey, cocoa powder, cinnamon and milk. Process all of the ingredients until a pudding forms.

Scrape all the pudding into a glass container and refrigerate. Try not to eat it all at once and do your best to share.

COCONUT WHIPPED CREAM DIRECTIONS: To make the coconut whipped cream, chill a can of full fat coconut milk in the fridge overnight. When you are ready to make the whipped cream, open up the can and scoop out the solid coconut milk fat and whip with a whisk or stand mixer. We do not feel the need to add any sweetener, but you could certainly add the honey if you wish. Dollop the whipped coconut cream on top of the mousse and enjoy!

SERVES 2

Banana Pancakes

These super simple banana and egg pancakes are fast, tasty, and totally Paleo. Ultra YUM!

2 bananas

4 eggs

pinch of cinnamon

pinch of nutmeg

splash of vanilla

coconut oil, enough to cover your cooking surface

You don't need to be super exact with spices; yesterday morning I accidentally loaded up on vanilla and they still tasted fantastic.

Note: The banana:egg ratio is 1:2. You can make a huge recipe or just enough for you.

Before you start blending or mixing, get out a pan, scoop out a big ol' spoonful of coconut oil and start heating it up. The oil should be just this side of smoking; water should DANCE if you flick a few tiny drops on to the surface.

Once you've got the oil heating up, blend everything else together in a cup or bowl 'till smooth.

We use an immersion blender we got for Christmas a few years back. Handy little things, we use it for everything from pancakes to buttered coffee.

Ok, back to the pancakes. Once you've got a smooth blend and a hot oiled cooking surface, start pouring out the pancakes. If you want this to be easy, do NOT make big pancakes. About the size of your palm or slightly larger is about as big as you want to go.

They'll be thin and should cook pretty quickly, a minute or two max on each side. Again, make sure your cooking surface is hot enough. If the batter doesn't "sizzle" as soon as it hits the pan, it's too cool. If the batter is super active when it hits and immediately bubbles up and gets brown, it's too hot.

At our house there are the quick and the hungry; wc usually cat 'em with our hands as soon as they're cool enough to touch. We recommend serving them hot to hungry people; you'll have a happy crowd.

SERVES 1

Nik's Butter Coffee

We're big fans of butter coffee and have been tweaking/perfecting this recipe for a few years. It's not rocket surgery, but there's more to it than just adding a chunk of butter and hoping that will work. It won't.

8 oz. hot coffee

PLACE THE FOLLOWING IN YOUR PRE-WARMED CUP:

1 Tbsp butter

1 Tbsp coconut oil

1 egg, raw (optional)

1 tsp collagen powder

OPTIONAL FOR MOCHA LOVERS

1 Tbsp cacao butter OR

1 tsp cacao powder

Pre-heat cup with hot water.

Remove hot water.

Place ingredients into cup.

Pour hot coffee on top of all the ingredients

Blend with an immersion blender.

Enjoy!

SERVES 6

Paleo Pizza Crust

From 11 year old fresh bakers to veteran Mamas, this gluten free pizza crust recipe has found success in every kitchen it's appeared in.

1 cup tapioca flour

1/4 - 1/2 tsp sea salt (your preference)

1/3 cup olive oil

1/3 cup water

1 Tbsp apple cider vinegar

1 egg

1/3 cup coconut flour

1 tsp Italian seasoning

Preheat oven to 450°F. If you are using a pizza stone, let the stone preheat with the oven.

In a medium bowl, add in tapioca flour, sea salt and Italian seasoning. Set aside.

In a small pot over medium heat, bring oil, water, and apple cider vinegar JUST up to boiling and then remove from heat. Add to your tapioca flour and stir until combined. Set aside for 1-2 minutes to cool.

Add in your egg and stir until combined.

Add in coconut flour and stir (or use your hands to mush it all together) until the coconut flour is absorbed and a dough is formed.

Press or roll out your dough on parchment paper or a lightly greased pizza stone or baking pan to about ¼" thickness. Your dough should form a 12-14" circle.

Slide your dough onto the pizza stone or baking sheet and cook for 9-10 minutes until the dough starts to brown slightly. Carefully flip the dough over and let it continue to cook for another 1-2 minutes while you gather your toppings.

Remove from oven; add your toppings and then bake for another 5 minutes or until your toppings are heated through.

SERVES 5

Seed + Nut Paleo Bread

Very little starch, mostly protein and fat. It is a crunchy dense bread that won't leaven. If you are expecting a "regular" doughy bread, this won't be for you. A little of this goes a long way because there is no starchy filler!

1 cup raw almonds

1 cup raw walnuts

3/4 cup chia seeds or flax seeds

3/4 cup raw sesame seeds

1 cup pepitas

1 cup raw sunflower seeds

1/3 cup coconut flour

5 eggs

1 1/2 tsp salt

Mix all ingredients together.

Put parchment paper in a bread pan. (I use a clay bread pan)

Pour ingredients in the pan.

Bake at 350°F degrees for 1 hour, check frequently.

I love it toasted, with butter and almond butter on top. A little goes a long way!

Peter SERVOLD

PETE'S PALEO FOUNDER

Peter Servold is the owner of Pete's Paleo, a nationally renowned Paleo company that cooks and ships ready-to-eat Paleo meals around the country, as well as sugar-free bacon and bone broth.

Peter has worked in the culinary and restaurant field nearly his whole life, from washing dishes to running front of house operations in multiple restaurants before attending culinary school. After attending Le Cordon Bleu, he worked at fine dining restaurants where he learned the true meaning of farm-to-table dining: working with the best possible ingredients, from the best local sources. From there he has managed restaurants, catering companies and restaurant consulting firms. Today he brings that experience and passion for real food to Pete's Paleo, providing fresh, Paleo-friendly meals to customers across the country.

www.petespaleo.com

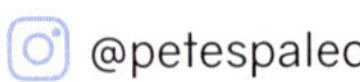

RECIPES

Baconnaise

Coffee Ice Cream

Lamb Quenelles

Pork Loin Wrapped in Bacon

Romanesco and Sweet Potatoes

SERVES 5

Baconnaise

1/2 cup bacon fat, in liquid form at room temperature

3/4 cup olive oil

2 large egg yolks

1 large whole egg

3/4 tsp salt

1 tsp apple cider vinegar

CHEF'S NOTE - While you can use a blender to make mayonnaise, I would only recommend that if you have a Vitamix or something of similar quality. Do not use a hand mixer— it will just make a huge mess.

Combine the bacon fat and oil in one measuring cup and set aside.

In a small metal bowl, use an immersion blender to blend (or whisk by hand) the egg yolks and whole egg until the mixture becomes milky white and frothy. When you see it change dramatically in color and texture, continue to mix a little longer. (This last bit of whisking is for added insurance, as it's at this stage that it's easy to stop blending too soon, and if the eggs aren't beaten enough, they cannot support the fat and emulsify into mayo.)

Once the eggs are the desired consistency, begin to slowly add the oil mixture.

Continue to mix until all the oil is added, about 1 to 2 minutes. Season with the salt and vinegar, and add more to taste as desired.

SERVES 5

Coffee Ice Cream

2 (13.5-ounce) cans unsweetened, whole-fat coconut milk or coconut cream

1/2 cup honey

1 Tbsp flavorless grass-fed gelatin

1 cup dark roast coffee grinds

In a medium saucepot over medium-low heat, warm the coconut milk very slowly so it doesn't separate. Once it gets warm, about 5 minutes, add the honey while whisking.

Continue to heat until the coconut and honey mixture is just below a simmer (180°F), about 10 minutes total. Add the gelatin and whisk until it's fully dissolved.

Once the mixture is at a good simmer (180°F to 195°F), pour it into a French press with the coffee grinds. Give it a good stir and allow to steep for 8 minutes. Strain it through a sieve held over a bowl.

Allow to cool in the fridge overnight. The next day, if the mixture has solidified, allow it to sit at room temperature for 30 minutes.

Pour into an ice cream maker and run for 25 minutes. Eat it right away if you like soft-serve or freeze it overnight for firm, scoopable ice cream. If you do freeze it, let it sit out for 5 to 10 minutes before serving for the perfect texture.

SERVES 4

Lamb Quenelles

1 pound (4 cups) braised lamb, warm

2 Tbsp chopped fresh parsley

1/2 cup shelled pistachios, raw and unsalted

1/4 cup bacon fat or any rendered animal fat, melted

1 large egg

olive or avocado oil, for frying (the exact amount depends on the pan)

salt to taste

FOR THE BATTER

1 large egg

2 Tbsp water

1 cup almond flour

In a food processor, pulse the still-warm meat and parsley for 30 seconds, then add the pistachios and process for an additional 30 seconds. With the processor running, slowly drizzle the warm fat into the processor. Continue processing until the mixture becomes dough-like—it should form into a ball that rotates around the processor. Add the egg and process for 15 to 30 seconds. Taste and season lightly with salt—remembering that the fat and the braised meat are already seasoned. (I suggest you start with 1/4 teaspoon salt and add more if needed.)

Quenelles can be formed two ways: The traditional, classic way, using two spoons, or the easy way, using an ice cream scoop. The ice cream scoop method works well, though the quenelles will not be as pretty as those formed using the classic method.

To form quenelles the easy way: Roll the edge of an ice cream scoop along the top of your mixture. Gently fill the scoop about halfway, forming a basic quenelle that can be now be put on a sheet tray to freeze.

To form them the classic way: Get two same-sized spoons and a cup of warm water. The size of the spoon determines the size of the quenelles; for this recipe, use a dinner spoon. With one spoon, scoop up a generous spoonful of the mixture (it's easier to form quenelles when there's more mixture in the spoon). Using the inside, concave surface of the other spoon, push the mixture back onto the opposite spoon while turning your hand around the lamb mixture, holding onto the angle and creating a sharp edge to the quenelle. Dip the first spoon into the warm water and push the mixture back into that spoon while rotating. Repeat a few times until the quenelle is formed. (It will look like a little football.)

This isn't the easiest thing to get down. I was mocked incessantly for my horrible quenelles at the restaurant where I worked under a sous chef (Eric Brown, a certified badass and now a great friend) who could quenelle a Muscat grape puree with his eyes closed better than I could with my eyes open—which he did just to prove how awful I was. But with practice you'll figure it out, and it's a skill you will have forever.

Chill the formed quenelles in the freezer for 25 minutes. Keep them separated on a sheet pan so they don't stick together. Don't skip this step; chilling the quenelles lets the egg wash and almond flour stick and keeps the lamb from overcooking when you fry it.

Once the quenelles have chilled, begin heating the oil. Fill a pan (I like to use a 12-inch cast iron pan) so the oil reaches 1/2 inch up the sides, and set it over medium heat.

In a medium bowl, whisk together the egg and the water. Place the flour in another bowl.

One by one, roll the quenelles in the egg mixture and then gently roll in the almond flour.

When the surface of the oil looks wavy and a couple pinches of almond flour fry up quickly, the oil is ready. (If you're checking with a thermometer, 325°F is the perfect temp.) Fry the quenelles for about 2 minutes per side, or until golden-brown. Transfer the finished ones to a plate lined with paper towels and hit them with a pinch of salt.

SERVES 4

Pork Loin Wrapped in Bacon

6 ounces bacon, thinly sliced

1 1/2 pounds pork tenderloin, cut into 5-ounce pieces about 2 inches thick

salt

CHEF'S NOTE - Blanching bacon is somewhat counter-intuitive, but it renders some of the fat, which helps the bacon crisp up and keeps it from shriveling, so it will wrap the tenderloin better. Plus, any time you blanch bacon, you create bacon stock, the perfect base for potato and leek soup.

Preheat the oven to 400°F.

Blanch the bacon for 3 minutes and lay it on a plate lined with paper towels.

Lightly sprinkle the pieces of tenderloin with salt and wrap it in the bacon.

Place the wrapped tenderloin in a cold, thick-bottomed, oven-safe sauté pan over medium-high heat. Start with the side with the bacon ends on the bottom of the pan so that it cooks first and the bacon ends seal closed. Cook for roughly 7 to 8 minutes on this side. Then rotate the tenderloin along its edge, cooking to a golden-brown all the way around. You should spend roughly 3 to 4 minutes on every side once the pan is nice and hot.

Transfer the pork loin to a roast rack, again with the bacon ends on the bottom, letting gravity help keep it together. Roast for approximately 9 minutes. If, like me, you prefer your pork cooked medium, around 140°F and with a medium-pink center, cook it for slightly less time—around 6 minutes is perfect.

Remove the pork from the oven and let it rest on a cutting board for 4 to 6 minutes. If you put a few paper towels down underneath the loin before cutting it, the runoff juices will be absorbed, saving you a mess on the board and, more importantly, on your pretty plate. Cut into ½-inch-thick slices, using a sharp slicing or chef's knife.

Pictured here with with Romanesco and Sweet Potatoes (see next recipe).

SERVES 4

Romanesco + Sweet Potatoes

1 head romanesco, cut into small florets (about 2 cups)

1 Tbsp olive oil

1/4 tsp salt

1 pound purple sweet potatoes, diced

1 Tbsp ghee

2 Tbsp chopped shallots

4 ounces chicken stock

CHEF'S NOTE: When working with romanesco, cut with care and go over it a few times—just a little extra work yields amazing results. It's best to cut it in a way that gets you the desired bite-sized pieces while retaining the natural beauty of the vegetable. This is done with a small paring knife and time. Using just the tip of the knife, cut off whole pieces of the romanesco and work from large to small, breaking it down to bite-sized pieces.

Blanching not only makes vegetables cook faster, it also helps their colors stay vibrant, keeps them moist during oven roasting, and helps them brown better in a sauté pan. It's perfect when you are cooking for a dinner party, since it lets you do most of the cooking in advance. After blanching, quickly roast or sear the vegetables before you put them on the plate.

Preheat oven to 400°F.

Blanch the romanesco for 3 minutes, dip it in an ice bath, and dry it in a colander. Lightly coat it with the olive oil and salt and place it on a sheet pan. Roast for 15 minutes—the romanesco will soften, but it will not start to turn golden-brown.

Blanch the sweet potatoes for 3 minutes, place in ice water for 2 to 3 minutes, and drain. They should be just shy of tender enough to eat. If you cut the potatoes into larger pieces, they'll need to cook a bit longer.

Heat the ghee in a large, thick-bottomed sauté pan over medium heat. Once the ghee is hot, add the shallots and sauté for 1 minute, then add the romaesco and sweet potatoes and sauté until tender, approximately 6 to 7 minutes.

While you sauté the vegetables, bring the stock to a simmer in a saucepan. As soon as you start to see some color and the vegetables are sticking to the bottom of the pan, add the simmering stock to the sauté pan. This will release the vegetables and the fond from the bottom of the pan.

Hayley MASON and Bill STALEY

PRIMAL PALATE FOUNDERS

Hayley Mason and Bill Staley are the duo behind the popular Paleo recipe website, Primal Palate. They are also the creators of Primal Palate Organic Spices - a premium line of ingredient-focused and Whole30 Approved spice blends that have become the sweetheart of Instagram foodies everywhere. Hayley and Bill are the authors of several bestselling Paleo cookbooks: *Make it Paleo* (1 & 2), *Gather*, and *The 30 Day Guide to Paleo Cooking*. Their Paleo journeys began in 2010 with their blog, and they have since grown to become two of the preeminent Paleo recipe developers. Known for their simple and delicious recipes as well as beautiful, bright photography, Hayley and Bill's recipes are instantly recognizable, whether they're on your phone screen or on your plate.

www.primalpalate.com

RECIPES

Clean Eatin' Buffalo Wings

Dairy-free Crème Brûlée

Jerk Shrimp Tacos with Mango Pomegranate Salsa

New Bae Fries

Easy Baked Chicken Tenders

SERVES 4

Clean Eatin' Buffalo Wings

This is, hands down, the easiest way to make Buffalo Wings! The tried and true ratio of Frank's Redhot to butter is 3:2. We're using clarified butter (*ghee) to clean this recipe up that much more! It's just as delicious!

4 lb chicken wings, cut into winglets

1/2 tsp Himalayan pink salt

3/4 cup hot sauce (Frank's Redhot), original flavor is Whole30 compliant

1/4 cup Tin Star Cultured Ghee, (add an additional 1/4 cup if you don't like the wings too spicy)

1/2 cup Primal Kitchen Mayonnaise

1 Tbsp coconut cream, from a can of full fat coconut milk

1 Tbsp lemon juice

1 Tbsp Primal Palate Organic Spices - Garden Ranch Seasoning Mix

To make the dip: Blend together the mayonnaise, coconut cream, lemon juice, and Garden Ranch Seasoning Mix.

Preheat your oven to 425°F.

Place a wire rack over a large, rimmed baking sheet.

If not already done, cut wings into winglets (save the wing tips for making stock).

Place wings on the wire rack with the thicker skin side up. Sprinkle lightly with pink Himalayan salt.

Bake wings for 40 minutes, until crisp and golden.

While wings are baking, bring together the sauce. Over medium low heat, melt the ghee and add the Frank's Redhot. Whisk to incorporate ghee into hot sauce.

Remove wings from oven, place in large bowl. Pour over the wing sauce and stir to coat.

Serve with some Whole30 compliant ranch (like Tessemae's) and some celery sticks.

SERVES 2

Dairy-free Crème Brûlée

The simple and decadent pleasure of a good crème brûlée is often associated with Valentine's Day, but this dessert should be enjoyed more than just once a year. With only 5 ingredients, this is a recipe that combines simplicity with sublime taste.

4 egg yolk

2 Tbsp maple sugar, (ideally, sifted or crushed fine)

200g coconut cream

1 tsp pure vanilla extract, or freshly scraped vanilla bean

1 tsp raw sugar, for the topping, must be fine granular

Preheat oven to 300°F, and boil a kettle of water

Separate 4 eggs, placing the yolks in a medium mixing bowl. The whites are not needed for this recipe.

Whisk in 2 tablespoons of maple sugar or other fine sugar. Set aside.

Measure 200g of coconut cream and place in a medium sauce pan. Heat over medium heat, and stir in 1 teaspoon of vanilla extract. If you have vanilla pods, scrape the vanilla beans from ½ of a vanilla pod. Stir to combine.

When the coconut cream comes to a soft boil, remove from heat, and incorporate into the eggs, little by little while whisking the eggs (this is called tempering; if you don't do this properly, you'll end up with sweet, scrambled eggs).

Pour the egg yolk cream mixture into two 4-oz ramekins. Place the filled ramekins into a baking dish, and then add boiling water around them, filling about half way up the ramekins.

Carefully transfer to a hot oven, and bake for 35-40 minutes. When they are done, the centers should still jiggle slightly.

Remove from heat, and allow the ramekins to cool 10 minutes before refrigerating at least 2 hours, ideally overnight.

Sprinkle any fine granulated sugar over the tops of the ramekins. Ensure your coverage is even, then torch with a kitchen torch. If you don't have a torch, you can also use your oven broiler, or a powerful stick lighter. Torch the sugar gently so that it does not burn. If a portion does burn, swirl the ramekin to distribute the darker colored sugar.

Allow to cool for a few minutes before serving. Enjoy!

SERVES 4

Jerk Shrimp Tacos with Mango Pomegranate Salsa

We LOVE shrimp tacos, and they are super tasty when you use Jerk Seasoning. This recipe for jerk shrimp tacos is light, and refreshing topped with our mango pomegranate salsa.

1 lb raw shrimp, large or jumbo, peeled and deveined

1 tsp Primal Palate Jerk Seasoning

1 Tbsp extra virgin olive oil

1 cup vine-ripened tomato, seeded and diced (1 large tomato)

1 cup green bell peppers, seeded and diced (1 bell pepper)

2/3 cup mango, peeled, and diced (1 mango)

2 Tbsp red onion, diced fine

1/3 cup pomegranate seeds

1 Tbsp lime juice, (juice of 1/2 lime)

1 pinch Himalayan pink salt

1 pinch cilantro for garnish

2 cups romaine lettuce, shredded

4 cassava flour tortillas (Siete)

In a medium size mixing bowl, combine the tomato, green bell pepper, mango, red onion, and pomegranate seeds.

Drizzle with olive oil and lime juice, and stir to combine evenly.

Add a pinch of salt, and chopped cilantro.

Heat a stainless steel skillet over medium heat with about a tablespoon of olive oil.

Add the shrimp to the skillet; cook on either side until they are pink, and no longer translucent, just a couple minutes per side.

Season with a teaspoon of Jerk Seasoning, and toss to combine evenly over the shrimp.

Warm the tortillas over a burner on the stove.

To plate, add some shredded lettuce, the shrimp, and top with the salsa. Add additional cilantro if desired.

SERVES 2

New Bae Fries

Fries are one of our all time favorite foods, and when you add some New Bae Seasoning to them, they are fiery and delicious! This technique for making fries is quick and easy. Enjoy our New Bae fries with some delicious, Paleo-friendly ketchup!

2 cups white potatoes, 2 medium to large potatoes

1 cup lard, or your choice of fat for frying

1 Tbsp Primal Palate New Bae Seasoning

Rinse and brush the potatoes. I like leaving the skin on, but you can also peel the potatoes.

Slice the potatoes into ½" - ¾" thick fries. The important thing is consistency of cut, so they all cook evenly.

Heat the cup of lard (or other cooking fat) over medium heat in a heavy skillet.

When the fat is heated, fry the potatoes. Fry for 3-4 minutes per side, allowing them to fry on each side at least once.

Remove from the pan, and allow to drain on a rack. Season with Primal Palate New Bae Seasoning immediately.

Serve hot with ketchup or your choice of condiments (the Primal Kitchen Chipotle Mayo is also great with fries!)

SERVES 2

Easy Baked Chicken Tenders

These easy and delicious baked chicken tenders are sure to please children and adults alike. They use just a few ingredients, but are full of flavor, and will keep you coming back for just one more bite!

8 whole chicken tenders

5 1/3 oz Kite Hill Greek Style Yogurt -plain unsweetened

4 1/4 oz Simple Mills Fine Ground Sea Salt Almond Flour Crackers

1 tsp Primal Palate Adobo Seasoning

1 Tbsp extra virgin olive oil, spray

Remove the tendon from your chicken tenders if desired, and place them in a gallon ziplock bag.

Pour the entire cup of Kite Hill Greek Style Plain Yogurt over the chicken.

Seal the gallon bag, and massage the yogurt into the chicken, being sure it coats all of the chicken. Place in the fridge to marinate for one hour.

Pour one box of Simple Mills Sea Salt Almond Flour crackers into a mini chop food processor.

Pulse the crackers until you have a fine meal.

Add one teaspoon of Primal Palate Adobo Seasoning if desired, and pulse again so that the seasoning is evenly distributed into the cracker meal.

Pour the cracker meal into a wide, shallow bowl.

Preheat your oven to 400°F, and place a wire rack over a baking sheet.

Remove the chicken tenders from the fridge.

Remove each tender, one at a time, and dredge in the cracker meal to evenly coat on all sides. Then place the breaded tender onto your baking sheet.

Repeat the dredging process until you have coated all of the tenders.

Using an olive oil spray, spritz the tenders lightly so they brown nicely in the oven.

Bake the tenders for 30 minutes, or until cooked thoroughly through the center, and golden brown on the outside.

Enjoy with your choice of condiments!

Robb WOLF

BESTSELLING AUTHOR

Robb Wolf, 2x New York Times bestselling author of *The Paleo Solution* and *Wired to Eat*, is a former research biochemist and one of the world's leading experts in ancestral health and lifestyle. Wolf has transformed the lives of hundreds of thousands of people around the world via his top ranked podcast, online course on the ketogenic diet, books, and seminar series. Outside of the ancestral world, you can find Robb rolling on Brazilian Jiu-Jitsu mats or spending quality time with his better half, Nicki, and their daughters.

www.robbwolf.com

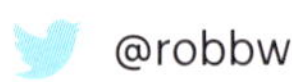

RECIPES

Nutty Hot Cereal

Simple Keto Fudge

NorCal Margarita

Killer Kale Salad

Instant Pot Soup

SERVES 1

Nutty Hot Cereal

1 cup almonds

1 apple, sliced

1-1.5 cups water

Blend almonds, apples, and water until smooth. Cook on the stove top for 5-10 minutes, just like hot cereal. You may need to add a bit more water to reach the desired consistency.

Garnish with cinnamon and enjoy! This cereal stores well, just cover and place in the refrigerator. Our girls like the cold cereal even more than the hot version.

SERVES 1

Simple Keto Fudge

2 cups heavy whipping cream

1/2 cup erythritol or sugar substitute of choice

6 oz unsweetened baking chocolate

dash of salt

Add heavy cream and erythritol to a saucepan and heat on low, stirring regularly. Bring to a low simmer, then remove from heat. Add the dark chocolate and salt and stir until the chocolate is thoroughly mixed.

Pour into 6" x 9" baking dish, silicone molds, ramekins, or fudgsicle pop molds. Put in freezer for 2-3 hours or until frozen. Remove from freezer about 10 minutes prior to serving.

Store in freezer or refrigerator.

SERVES 1

NorCal Margarita

This recipe began in our Chico gym where our clients needed a drink that supported their socializing without thwarting their progress. No sugar but bursting with "yum", the NorCal Margarita was the drink that became an international sensation.

2-3 oz of 100% agave tequila

juice and pulp from one lime

ice

soda water, to taste

Mix tequila and lime juice in a shaker.

Add ice and shake!

Pour in glass over ice.

Top it off with a splash of soda water (or more, if you want to dilute it down a bit).

To really feel like you're on a tropical beach, garnish with lime, lemon, and/or orange slices.

Enjoy!

SERVES 1

Killer Kale Salad

This is a staple at the Wolf household. It's easy to make and a crowd pleaser!

1 bunch kale

2-3 medium cloves garlic

3/4 cup olive oil

2 Tbsp lemon juice

3-4 Tbsp grated Parmesan cheese (optional)

15 cracks black pepper

1/8 tsp salt

Pick leaves off the kale stems and toss in a salad spinner. Wash leaves thoroughly, then spin out the water. Place in a salad bowl. Sprinkle with parmesan cheese if using.

THE DRESSING: Add the olive oil, garlic, lemon juice, salt and pepper to a blender and blend thoroughly, about 60 seconds. Pour over the salad, toss, and enjoy!

Robb Wolf

SERVES 1

Instant Pot Soup

I love soup. ANY soup. Folks often dismiss this aqueous delight in favor of what they perceive to be more substantial fare, but don't underestimate the power and flavor of "stuff boiled in water." You can make soup in a wide variety of vessels, but my favorite method the past few years has been the Instant Pot. This nifty kitchen accoutrement allows one to cook meals over the course of hours using the "slow cooker settings" or in minutes by shifting to the pressure cooker. It's up to you how you do this but the flexibility is amazing. If I'm on top of my day I'll prep the soup around noon and let it slow cook until we eat around 4:30 or 5:00 pm. If the day got away from me, I can get all this into the pot at 3:30 or 4:00, pressure cook it for 20 minutes and the Wolf pack is ready to grub.

1 large can of diced tomatoes

2 lbs of ground meat, beef or turkey

3-4 medium zucchini

3-4 large carrots

1 large onion

salt and pepper to taste

1 Tbsp garlic powder

bone broth or water

Empty the can of diced tomatoes into the Instant Pot. Break up the ground meat and mix this into the tomatoes, making a "pink goo" type consistency.

Dice or put through a food processor the remaining vegetables and add to the pot, mixing thoroughly.

Add bone broth or water to bring the pot to a desired level and season with salt and garlic powder to taste. If you have lots of time, slow cook for 3-4 hours, if you are time crunched, pressure cook for 20 minutes.

MAKE SURE to adjust the venting device to the proper setting on your Instant Pot!

Sarah FRAGOSO

BESTSELLING AUTHOR

Eleven years ago, a new lifestyle emerged for Sarah that created some much needed positive momentum. After struggling with numerous health issues preceding the birth of her 3rd child, Sarah regained her health and began to share her journey with others when she started her blog and brand, Everyday Paleo. Sarah was the first woman to blog about living an ancestral lifestyle. She became an overnight Internet sensation, reaching millions around the globe with her inspiring message and delicious recipes. Sarah has since become an International Best Selling Author of five books. She blogs exclusively at SarahFragoso.com, communicates through a thriving social media platform, and conducts consistently sold-out seminars and retreats. She is a certified personal trainer, certified mindfulness coach, and is co-owner of a Chico, CA based gym, JS Strength & Conditioning. For the last 8 years, Sarah has also been a top ten iTunes podcaster with her current new podcast hit, Better Everyday With Sarah & Dr Brooke, ranking in at number 2 in Alternative Health on the very first day of it's release. Her next highly anticipated book Hangry, a 4 week fully customizable hormone-healing health plan for women, and co-authored by Dr. Brooke Kalanick, N.D., is scheduled to come out June 4th of 2019.

www.sarahfragoso.com

/therealsarahfragoso @sarah_fragoso

RECIPES

Jaden's Flan

Seafood and Veggie Chowder

Simple Seasonal Soup

Spanish Meatballs

Zesty Cabbage Slaw with Cumin + Lime Dressing

Sarah Fragoso

SERVES 6

Jaden's Flan

1 1/2 cups full fat canned coconut milk

1 cups heavy cream (if you are dairy free simply use 2 1/2 total cups of coconut milk)

4 eggs

1 tsp vanilla extract

2 Tbsp honey for flan

1/4 cup honey to caramelize

squeeze of lemon juice (about 1 tsp)

1 Tbsp water

*Top with sliced strawberries and blueberries if desired

Preheat oven to 350°F.

Combine the coconut milk, heavy cream if using, eggs, vanilla, and 2 tablespoons of honey into a blender and blend until mixed well.

In a small saucepan add the tablespoon of water, the squeeze of lemon juice and the ¼ cup of honey over low to medium low heat. Bring to a simmer, stirring occasionally until the mixture is golden brown, approximately 8 minutes, remove from heat immediately (note: do not stir and/or cook too long because the honey will crystalize and be sure to remove from the heat as soon as you see the change in color)

Immediately pour the honey mixture into the bottom of a 2-quart round baking dish or soufflé pan and tilt the dish/pan until the bottom is coated and let cool for 3-4 minutes. Gently pour the coconut milk mixture on top of the honey.

Place the round pan with the flan mixture into a larger baking dish and pour in enough hot water so that the water is about an inch deep. Bake uncovered at 350°F for 50-60 minutes or until the flan is set in the middle and a custard like texture. Cool for at least 30 minutes in the refrigerator before serving.

SERVES 4

Seafood + Veggie Chowder

- 2 garlic cloves, minced
- 6 bacon strips, chopped
- 3 celery stalks, diced
- 1 pound Brussels sprouts, quartered
- 4 cups chicken broth
- 1 cup coconut milk or heavy cream
- 1 small red bell pepper, diced
- 2 carrots, chopped
- 1 Tbsp dried dill
- 1 Tbsp red chili flakes (optional)
- sea salt and black pepper to taste
- 2 pounds fresh wild caught salmon, cod, or other seafood of your choice cut into bite sized pieces

Add the bacon to a large soup pot and brown over medium-to-medium high heat.

Once the bacon starts to crisp, add the onions and sauté until the onions become translucent.

Add the garlic and celery and sauté until the garlic is fragrant.

Add the chicken broth and coconut milk or heavy cream and bring to a boil.

Add the quartered Brussels sprouts and carrots and simmer until the veggies are tender but not mushy.

Add the red bell peppers and seafood and cook just until the fish flakes apart easily or if using shrimp or prawns, until they turn pink.

Season with the dill and salt and pepper to taste and add the red chili flakes if desired.

Serve immediately.

SERVES 4 - 5

Simple Seasonal Soup

This is an example of a summer soup; if it's winter and you do not have access to fresh corn I recommend subbing with cubed winter squash or sweet potatoes. The point is, you can make this soup all year long, just mix up the veggies based on the season!

SOUP BASE

8-10 cups chicken bone broth

1 - 2 lbs. shredded cooked chicken thighs (Cook in your instant pot for 14 minutes under high pressure with 1/4 cup liquid. Another easy way to cook the chicken thighs is to place them in a small pot and cover with some of the chicken broth, bring to a boil and turn down to a simmer for approximately 40 minutes for bone in thighs and 15-20 for boneless thighs. Once the juices run clear and the meat easily shreds, the chicken is done. Shred the chicken and set aside until it's time to add to the soup)

1 small yellow onion, diced

1 red bell pepper, diced

4 Tbsp extra virgin olive oil

2-4 garlic cloves, minced

3 ears of organic sweet corn (optional)

2 medium yellow summer squash or zucchini

5-6 oz of your favorite greens (I suggest spinach or baby kale)

1-2 Tbsp ground cumin

1-2 Tbsp dried oregano

Juice from two limes (or to taste)

1/2 - 1 tsp chipotle or ancho chili powder (I suggest chipotle for the smoky flavor)

sea salt and black pepper to taste

TOPPINGS

1 jicama, peeled and diced

1 bunch of cilantro, chopped

5-6 radishes, halved and thinly sliced

4-5 green onions, chopped

1-2 avocados, peeled and diced

crumbled cotija cheese (omit if you avoid dairy)

1 lime, sliced

Add the olive oil to the bottom of a large soup pot and heat over medium heat. Add the onion and bell pepper, season with a little sea salt, and sauté until the onions and peppers are soft.

Add the minced garlic and sauté just until the garlic is fragrant.

Slowly pour in the chicken broth and bring to a simmer.

While you are waiting for your broth to simmer, cut the kernels off your ears of corn.

Add the fresh corn and the yellow summer squash or zucchini to the broth and let cook for 5-7 minutes.

Add the already cooked shredded chicken, greens, the spices, lime juice, and salt and pepper to taste and let simmer another 5-7 minutes.

Check your seasoning and add more cumin, oregano, salt, pepper, and/or lime juice per your personal taste preference! This soup should be bursting with flavor!

To serve, ladle a big ol' serving into your soup bowl and top heartily with all of your toppings, finishing with a generous sprinkle of the cotija cheese if desired.

Enjoy and eat the leftovers for breakfast and or lunch the next day!

SERVES 6

Spanish Meatballs

MEATBALLS

2 lbs grass fed ground beef

1 lb pasture raised ground pork

1 egg

4 garlic cloves, minced

1/4 cup minced fresh flat leaf parsley

2 tsp cumin powder

1 1/2 tsp smoked paprika

2 1/2 tsp sea salt

1 tsp black pepper

SAUCE

1 Tbsp extra virgin olive oil

1 yellow onion, cut in half and sliced

3-4 garlic cloves, minced

1/2 cup white wine

28 oz. can of diced organic tomatoes

1 cup Spanish olives

2 Tbsp minced fresh parsley

1 tsp smoked paprika

1/4 tsp cayenne

1/4 tsp or one pinch saffron

lemon

salt and freshly ground pepper to taste

MEATBALLS: Combine all meatball ingredients together in a large bowl and mix with your hands.

Using a ⅓ cup measuring cup, measure out the meat into even sized meatballs.

SAUCE: First prepare the saffron water:
Toast the saffron strands in a warm skillet over low heat for 1 minute.

Add the toasted saffron strands into a ¼ cup hot water and set aside.

Heat the olive oil over medium heat, add the sliced onions, and sauté for 5-7 minutes or until translucent.

Add the garlic and sauté just until the garlic is fragrant.

Turn the heat up to high and add the white wine and reduce by ½, stirring occasionally.

Add the saffron water and tomatoes and bring to a simmer.

Add the remaining ingredients and season to taste with a little lemon juice, salt and pepper.

Gently nestle the meatballs into the sauce, turn down to low or medium low and simmer covered for 15 – 20 minutes until meatballs are cooked through and tender.

SERVES 4

Zesty Cabbage Slaw with Cumin + Lime Dressing

4 cups chopped or shredded green cabbage

2 green onions, chopped

1 small cucumber, diced

2 radishes, cut in half and thinly sliced

1 cup diced jicama

1/2 cup cilantro leaves, chopped

*dress to taste with Cumin & Lime Dressing.

CUMIN AND LIME DRESSING

1/3 cup avocado oil

juice from 1 lime

1 1/2 tsp ground cumin

1/4 tsp smoked paprika

pinch of cayenne pepper

sea salt and pepper to taste

Toss together all the salad ingredients in a bowl and set aside.

In a small bowl whisk together the ingredients for the dressing.

Dress the salad to taste with the Cumin and Lime Dressing and serve immediately.

Forbes RILEY

CELEBRITY HEALTH & FITNESS EXPERT

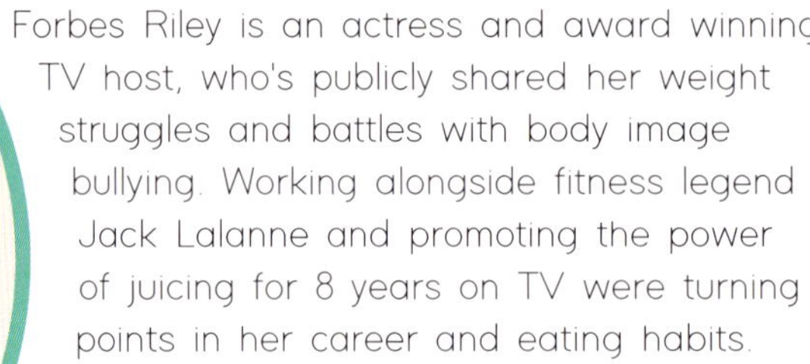

Forbes Riley is an actress and award winning TV host, who's publicly shared her weight struggles and battles with body image bullying. Working alongside fitness legend Jack Lalanne and promoting the power of juicing for 8 years on TV were turning points in her career and eating habits.

Her drive to help others transform their health has not only resulted in more than $2.5 Billion dollars in product sales via infomercials and home shopping, but got her inducted into the National Fitness Hall of Fame.

Combined with her signature handheld fitness device called the SpinGym, Forbes continues on her mission to help millions on THEIR path to wellness through diet and exercise.

Her weekly podcast, The Forbes Factor, focusing on health, wealth and happiness, just celebrated its 10th Anniversary and her latest, best-selling book, *What Have You Forbes'd Lately?* illuminates the power of entrepreneurship and manifesting your dreams into reality.

Forbes can be seen as a motivational speaker on stages around the globe...that is, when she's not at home in St Petersburg, Florida with her teenage boy/girl twins!

Forbes works closely with her personal chef Sharon Guerin. Together, the two have developed these Forbes Favorites, enjoy 'em in your kitchen!

Sharon GUERIN

THE CULINARY QUEEN

Self taught and killin' it, Sharon has been cooking since age 9. She specializes in a healthy take on classic dishes with gluten free and keto friendly meals that don't take the comfort out of comfort food recipes. Sharon loves creating custom dishes, from private chef clients to catering large events.

Sharon attended www.ForbesFactorLive.com as a student and became a personal chef and dear friend of Forbes, inspiring new healthy recipes that they both eat and share with friends regularly.

www.forbesriley.com

/forbesrileyfanpage

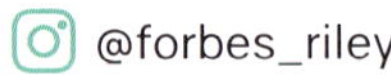

@forbes_riley

@forbesriley

RECIPES

"Kids-On-The-Go" Protein Pancake

Summer Salad with Champagne Dressing

Seared Scallops with Mushroom Risotto + Roasted Asparagus and Blistered Tomatoes

Filet Mignon with Butternut Squash Mash + Roasted Carrots

Vivid Vanilla Crème Brûlée

SERVES 2

"Kids-On-The-Go" Protein Pancake

With growing twins and a busy career, this is our GO-TO breakfast, snack and sometimes even dinner! Don't let the 3 simple ingredients fool you: Packed with nutrition, without flour or gluten, this comfort food staple meal is ideal whether you're on a diet or just focusing on eating healthy.

4 scoops of your favorite protein powder (vanilla, chocolate, cinnamon all work!)

2 eggs

1 cup of unsweetened almond milk

1 Tbsp of grass-fed butter

Mix all ingredients together in a bowl and whisk until smooth.

Heat non-stick pan or griddle. Grease cooking surface with butter.

Pour mix on cooking surface and wait for the top to bubble.

Flip. Remove when the edges begin to lift.

For variety, you can add in or serve with:
· Bananas
· Chocolate Chips
· Grade A Maple Syrup
· Confectioners Sugar
· Organic Peanut Butter
· Organic Apple Sauce

SERVES 1 - CROWD

Summer Salad with Champagne Dressing

While a salad may just be a salad, your mouth will truly water when you top these greens with Sharon's award-winning Champagne Mustard Vinaigrette Salad Dressing. It's so good, she's determined to bottle it! So shush, we've given you the secret ingredients here and you MUST try it!

SALAD

- organic super greens salad mix
- orange medallions
- organic edamame peas
- sunflower seeds
- dried cranberries
- sliced almonds
- organic avocado slices

CMV DRESSING

- 1/4 organic Champagne vinegar
- 1/2 cup of avocado oil
- 1 large garlic clove
- 2 Tbsp of organic Dijon mustard
- 1 Tbsp of lime juice
- 3 Tbsp of organic raw honey
- 1/2 tsp of Himalayan salt
- 1/2 tsp of cracked black pepper

SALAD: Mix all the ingredients based on the amount of people you are feeding. The great thing about this salad is it is fresh, light and healthy. You can make it for one or a crowd!

CMV DRESSING: Combine all ingredients in your blender and blend until smooth and serve. You can keep this in your refrigerator up to a week. Shake, use and enjoy!

SERVES 4

Seared Scallops with Mushroom Risotto + Roasted Asparagus and Blistered Tomatoes

Risotto is one of those foods that I hate to love. Traditionally made with Arborio rice, it's starchier than most other types of rice. Sharon taught me the secret of substituting cauliflower. The texture is creamy, the taste out of this world, and when you pair it with deliciously grilled scallops and top it off with roasted tomatoes and asparagus you'll have a culinary treat that's to DIVE FOR!

ROASTED ASPARAGUS w/ BLISTERED COLORED CHERRY TOMATOES

ASPARAGUS

1 bunch of asparagus

avocado oil

2 cloves of garlic

Himalayan salt

black pepper

TOMATOES

one pack of colored cherry tomatoes

one shallot

2 cloves of garlic

Himalayan salt

black pepper

CAULIFLOWER MUSHROOM RISOTTO

1 head of cauliflower

8 oz portobello mushrooms

2 Tbsp avocado oil

1/2 stick of grass fed butter

1/4 cup of fresh cut herbs (thyme, rosemary and sage)

1 shallot

2 lemons

2 cups of organic vegetable stock

1 cup of heavy whipping cream

2 cups of grass fed Parmesan cheese

Himalayan salt

black pepper

PAN SEARED SCALLOPS

1 lb of dry sea scallops

2 Tbsp

avocado oil

1 Tbsp grass fed butter

Himalayan salt

black pepper

ROASTED ASPARAGUS w/ BLISTERED COLORED CHERRY TOMATOES:

Preheat oven to 375 degrees.

On a sheet pan, cut the white ends off the

asparagus and place them on one end of the pan. Drizzle with avocado oil. Mince two garlic cloves and sprinkle pink salt and black pepper to taste. Massage asparagus with hands until they're evenly coated.

On the other half of the sheet pan, cut the tomatoes in half. Mince the garlic and dice the shallot on to the top of the tomatoes. Drizzle with avocado oil.

Bake for 25 mins.

CAULIFLOWER MUSHROOM RISOTTO: Dice herbs, cauliflower and mushrooms until they are small and fine. Place to the side.

In a large skillet, heat avocado oil, butter, herbs and shallots. Sauté all of those ingredients until the shallots are translucent and soft (about 4 to 5 mins).

Add the diced cauliflower and mushrooms to pan and sauté until both are soft. Cut and squeeze the juice of two lemons over the pan and stir. When the lemon juice liquid is reduced, add the organic vegetable stock and reduce the heat. KEEP STIRRING. Stirring is as important with a vegetable risotto as it is with a rice risotto. When the liquid reduces to half or less, add the heavy whipping cream and stir! STIRRING IS IMPORTANT. Add salt and pepper to taste. When cream is thick and melding with the cauliflower and mushrooms, add the cheese and stir! Reduce heat and let simmer for 6 to 8 mins.

PAN SEARED SCALLOPS: Heat avocado oil in your still lightly oiled and slightly smoky cast iron skillet.

Pat dry the scallops. Salt and pepper each side to taste.

Place scallops in hot skillet. Let it sear until they don't stick to the pan, about 3 mins. Flip scallops. Add butter to the pan and baste while second side sears, about another 3 mins. Take out of skillet and rest.

DRESSING YOUR PLATE: Place one spoonful of the risotto down the middle of the plate. Add 8 to 10 spears of asparagus on one side and topped with blistered cherry tomatoes. Place scallops on the other side of the plate.

Serve.

SERVES 2-4

Filet Mignon w/ Butternut Squash Mash and Roasted Carrots

When Sharon and I talked about what recipes are important to us, we also shared WHY certain foods were important to us. For me, my grandfather was a butcher, and even though I went vegetarian for many years, steak holds a fond place in my heart. Sharon and I agree about 2 things: Steak must be rare and the best quality grass-fed beef! Today, neither of us eat much red meat, but when we do, this recipe is must... make no misSTEAK!

ROASTED CARROTS

4 cups of mini organic rainbow carrots

avocado oil

Himalayan salt

black pepper

BUTTERNUT SQUASH MASH

1 butternut squash cut and cleaned into cubes or 5 cups of pre-cut butternut squash

1 cup of cheddar cheese from grass fed cows

1/2 cup of organic heavy whipping cream

Himalayan salt

black pepper

FILET MIGNON

grass fed filet mignon (purchase the amount of steaks for people eating)

Himalayan salt and black pepper

2 Tbsp of avocado oil

2 Tbsp of grass fed butter

2 Tbsp of fresh cut herbs (thyme, rosemary and sage)

ROASTED CARROTS: Preheat oven to 375 degrees.

On a sheet pan lay out your carrots, drizzle avocado oil on the carrots, then sprinkle with pink salt and black pepper to taste. Massage the oil and seasoning onto the carrots, then place in the oven for 45 mins to 1 hour. The carrots should look golden brown and caramelized when done.

BUTTERNUT SQUASH MASH: Boil squash until tender, but not mushy. Drain and place in a

mixing bowl. Add cheese and heavy cream. Salt and pepper to taste. Mix together with a beater until creamy, with a similar consistency to mashed potatoes!

FILET MIGNON: In a cast iron skillet heat oil till your pan begins to smoke lightly.

Allow steak(s) to set on the counter and become room temperature. Pat dry with a paper towel to take the extra moisture out, this helps with proper searing.

Salt and pepper both sides of your steaks generously and massage in.

Place your steaks in the skillet and let sit for 3 to 4 mins. (If the steak sticks to the skillet when you go to turn, it is not ready. The steak won't stick when it is perfectly seared.)

Flip your steaks when you do this. After 2 mins add your grass fed butter and fresh cut herbs and begin to baste your steak. Do this for another 2 to 3 mins and remove from pan to cutting board and let your steak rest for 5 mins.

Plate your plate with butternut squash mash. Place the steak on the mash and dress with the carrots on the side of your steak.

SERVES 6

Vivid Vanilla Crème Brûlée

I first tasted Créme Brûlée (softly set custard with a mirror-smooth top of hard caramelized sugar) at a girlfriend's wedding in my 20's and my mouth melted... I've been obsessed ever since.
If you've never tried it...this recipe is a MUST!! In fact, while we were doing the photo shoot for this book, I ate 2 cups full! Sharon originally showed me her recipe that's near and dear to her heart because it uses her mother's organic vanilla from Mexico. Though her mom is no longer here, we can pass along a bit of her sweetness. So while you CAN get vanilla in most stores, I recommend seeking out a very high quality, as the flavor and purity of the vanilla will make this treat one that you too will remember forever.

2 cups of organic heavy whipping cream

6 egg yolks from organic brown free-range chicken

1/2 cup of organic pure cane sugar

1 1/2 Tbsp of organic pure vanilla

SPECIAL EQUIPMENT REQUIRED

Ramekins and a restaurant quality torch, both found at your local food specialty stores.

Preheat oven to 375 degrees.

Mix together the egg yolks, sugar and vanilla until creamy and smooth.

While mixing your egg mixture together, put your heavy whipping cream on the stove and heat until there's a slow boil just around the edges of the pot.

Do not allow cream to heavy boil or over boil.

When the cream is warm, remove from stove and pour it down the side of the mixed egg bowl, being sure not to pour cream directly on mixture (as this will cause premature cooking of the egg yolks). Whisk briskly as you pour. Continue to whisk until all the cream and egg mixture is smooth and slightly frothy.

Put your cream in a measuring cup and distribute mixture evenly into six baking ramekins. Place the ramekins into a pyrex baking dish, then fill the dish half-way with water (water bath the ramekins).

Bake for approximately 45 mins. Creme Brulee is done when they are golden brown and are jello-like to the touch. Take out of the oven and cool on the counter for a half hour, then refrigerate for at least two hours.

Cover the top of the custard with organic pure cane sugar and melt the sugar with a restaurant quality torch.

Garnish with fresh fruit.

Tony KASANDRINOS

KASANDRINOS.COM FOUNDER

Tony is a native of Rochester New York, but also spent a good portion of his childhood in his father's village Niata, in Greece. Upon graduating the Aquinas Institute, he joined the Marine Corps in October of 1997 where he served until retiring in 2019. Tony's duties have taken him all around the globe. On his free time, he enjoys being outdoors, hanging out with family and traveling (especially to Greece.)

www.kasandrinos.com

f /kasandrinosinternation

@kasandrinos

RECIPES

Baklava

Greek Fries

KEVOO Olives

Thea Fifi's Zucchini Balls

Tony's Lamb Chops

SERVES 2

Baklava

1 pack of coconut wraps

1 lb walnuts chopped

8 Tbsp coconut sugar

1/2 tsp cinnamon

1/4 tsp ground clove

1 lb unsalted butter

5 whole cloves

FOR SYRUP

4 cups coconut sugar

2 lemon slices

1 tsp lemon juice

2 sticks cinnamon

1 cup honey

Mix walnuts, coconut sugar, cinnamon, ground clove and 4 tablespoons melted butter in a bowl.

Butter pan liberally. Lay 2 layers of coconut wraps and butter each one well. Make sure to split filling into 5 parts. Evenly add ⅕ of the filling, then lay 1 layer of well buttered coconut wrap on top (repeat until filling is gone).

For the top layer, butter and lay each of the 2 sheets of coconut wraps, make sure to butter the top layer well too. Wet hands and sprinkle a little water on top.

Score the baklava with the knife only halfway through (don't cut through the bottom). After scoring, press 1 whole clove into the top of each piece.

Bake for about a 1 hour at 350°F.

SYRUP DIRECTIONS: Add everything except the honey to a pot and boil for 10 minutes.

Add honey and boil for 5 more minutes.

When baklava has cooled down and the syrup is STILL HOT pour over baklava.

SERVES 2

Greek Fries

4 russet potatoes

6-7 Tbsp Kasandrinos Extra Virgin Olive Oil

3-4 Tbsp Greek Balanced Bites Spice Blend

1 and 1/2 lemons

Preheat oven to 400°F. Peel potatoes. Cut potatoes in half-lengthwise and then in to ¼ inch thick wedges. Cut each wedge in half. Place potatoes, extra virgin olive oil, Greek Spice Blend, and the juice of one lemon in a bowl. Toss potatoes until they are evenly coated.

Line baking sheet with parchment paper and place potatoes in a single layer. Place baking sheet in oven and cook for 30-35 minutes on first side. Flip potatoes ensuring they are in an even layer and cook for another 10 minutes or until golden brown and fork tender.

Remove from oven, squeeze ½ a lemon on the fries and serve!

SERVES 2

KEVOO Olives

1 lb medium-large olives with pits (Kalamata olives recommended)

4 cups Kasandrinos Extra Virgin Olive Oil

1 lemon

1.5 Tbsp dried oregano

1/4 cup red wine vinegar

Individually score each olive from top to bottom. 3 scores per olive recommended depending on size.

Cut lemon into small wedges.

Combine extra virgin olive oil, oregano, and red wine vinegar.

Place lemon wedges and olives into a resealable and air tight container.

Pour extra virgin olive oil, oregano, and red wine vinegar mixture over lemon wedges and olives, ensuring all olives are covered.

Close container, ensure it is air tight, and place in a cool, dark place for a minimum of one to two weeks.

Tip: Marinate for 2 months for maximum flavor.

ORGANIC
VIRGIN OLIVE OIL
CERTIFIED ORGANIC
COLD EXTRACTION

SERVES 4

Thea Fifi's Zucchini Balls

- 2 zucchini
- 1/4 lb Greek feta
- 3 Tbsp chopped fresh dill
- salt
- pepper
- 1/4 cup mint leaves - packed
- 1 egg
- 1/4 cup cassava flour
- 1/3 cup Kasandrinos Extra Virgin Olive Oil

Finely grate zucchini using either a microplane or smallest setting on grater.

Place shredded zucchini in a cheese cloth and wring several times to remove all liquid.

Leave shredded zucchini in the cheese cloth and place the cheese cloth in a strainer for at least 2 hours to allow for any additional liquid to strain.

Chop mint and dill. Crumble feta.

Remove zucchini from the cheese cloth and place in a mixing bowl.

Add mint, dill, cassava flour, egg, salt and pepper to taste, and feta to shredded zucchini.

Mix all ingredients until evenly combined.

Shape mixture into 1" round balls.

Heat extra virgin olive oil in a frying pan on medium heat. Do not allow oil to smoke.

Place zucchini balls into frying pan being careful not to overcrowd the pan and fry each side until golden brown.

Place zucchini balls on a paper towel to drain excess oil and season with salt while hot.

Transfer to serving dish and enjoy!

SERVES 2

Tony's Lamb Chops

12 lamb rib chops – (3/4 inch thick; frenched)

6 Tbsp Kasandrinos Extra Virgin Olive Oil

2 Tbsp sea salt

1 Tbsp pepper

2 Tbsp dried oregano

1 lemon

Brush each lamb chop with extra virgin olive oil. Season each side with salt, pepper, and oregano. Refrigerate for 1 hour.

Remove from refrigerator and allow lamb chops to come up to room temperature prior to cooking to allow for even cook and sear.

Preheat oven to 400°F.

Place 4-5 tablespoons extra virgin olive oil in a pan, preferably a cast iron. Heat oil on medium to high heat.

Once extra virgin olive oil is warm, place lamb in pan and cook for 1.5 minutes on each side. Note: You may need to do this in batches depending on the size of your pan.

Place pan with lamb in oven for 7 minutes at 400°F for medium. Cook for less time to achieve medium rare.

Remove lamb from pan to stop cooking and rest meat for 5-7 minutes.

Squeeze lemon on chops and serve.

Vanessa BARAJAS

CLEAN EATING WITH A DIRTY MIND FOUNDER

Self-taught pastry chef Vanessa Barajas wants to bake the world a better place, one recipe at a time. Vanessa is the dessertavore behind the popular blog Clean Eating with a Dirty Mind. She believes that part of a healthy lifestyle is enjoying life. To her, enjoying life involves the occasional splurge or two.

All of Vanessa's stunning recipes are gluten-free and Paleo friendly, with one core principal - just because your food is healthy, doesn't mean it has to taste that way! After a 30-day Paleo challenge in 2013, Vanessa realized what a huge impact proper diet had on the body; she felt so great she never looked back. After trying tons of Paleo dessert recipes on the internet and being constantly disappointed with them, she took matters into her own hands. Intent on creating recipes that actually tasted like their unhealthy counterparts, she taught herself everything she could in her little tiny kitchen and started sharing her recipes with the world.

Vanessa is a San Diego native who loves food with an insane passion. She's been known to drink almond milk straight from the carton and expensive wine out of plastic red cups. Her favorite meal is, has, and always will be dessert.

www.cleaneatingwithadirtymind.com

/cleaneatingwithadirtymind

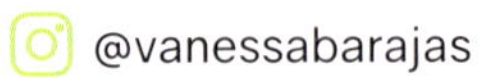
@vanessabarajas

@cleandirtyeats

RECIPES

Cookie Dough Fudge

Inside-Out Peanut Butter Cups

Molten Chocolate Lava Cake

Pumpkin Bread

Simple Chocolate Chip Cookies

SERVES 16 PIECES

Cookie Dough Fudge

8 Tbsp (4 ounces) salted butter

3 cups raw cashew pieces

1 Tbsp melted coconut oil

1/4 cup coconut flour

1/4 cup raw honey, melted

1/2 tsp fine-grain sea salt

1/2 tsp vanilla extract

1/8 tsp ground cinnamon or ground nutmeg

1 cup (3 1/2 ounces) chocolate chips

Line a 5"x 9" or 1 ½-quart, loaf pan with parchment paper; set aside.

Brown the butter by putting it in a medium-sized heavy-bottomed saucepan over medium-low heat. Stir intermittently using a rubber spatula. As the butter melts, it will start to bubble and foam. As it continues to cook, it will turn from lemon yellow to amber in color and will go from a loud bubble to a quiet simmer. When the butter is ready, brown specks will have formed at the bottom of the pan, and some of the specks will start to rise in the foam. The butter will also have a pleasant nutty aroma. Remove the pan from the heat and let cool for 15 to 20 minutes, until the pan is cool to the touch. When transferring the browned butter from the saucepan, be sure to use a rubber spatula to scrape all the browned bits of the bottom of the pan—that's where a lot of the flavor is.

Put the cashews into the bowl of a high-powered food processor and process until the cashews turn to meal. Scrape down the bowl and continue to process for another 5 minutes or so, stopping to scrape down as needed, until the nut oils start to release. With the processor on, slowly drizzle the melted coconut oil into the cashew meal and continue to process until it turns into a thick dough ball or attains a doughlike consistency (it will be much thicker and drier looking than peanut butter).

In a medium-sized bowl, combine the cashew butter, browned butter, and coconut flour and

stir together using an electric mixer or whisk. Next add the honey, salt, vanilla, and cinnamon and stir until combined and smooth. Press plastic wrap across the surface of the dough and freeze for 20 minutes. Then fold in chocolate chips. If the chocolate chips are added before, they will melt and sink to the bottom.

Transfer the dough to the parchment-lined pan and press it down evenly into the bottom. Place back in the freezer for 20 minutes to firm up and set. Cut into 16 pieces before serving. Store any remaining fudge in the freezer; remove from the freezer a few minutes before serving to thaw slightly.

NOTES Subs: Ghee in place of butter. Ghee doesn't brown since it's already clarified butter so I recommend using Tin Star Foods Browned Butter Ghee. For chocolate chips I recommend Guittard which are soy and dairy-free.

SERVES 9 CUPS

Inside-Out Peanut Butter Cups

1 cup creamy salted peanut butter or almond butter

1/4 cup melted coconut oil

2 Tbsp melted raw honey

1/2 cup chocolate chips

1/4 cup canned full-fat coconut milk

Line a 12-cup cupcake pan with 9 silicone baking liners. Set aside. Heat peanut butter in a microwave safe dish for 45 seconds to 1 minute or until it has a semi-liquid consistency and becomes pourable. Slowly drizzle the melted coconut oil into the heated peanut butter while stirring. Then mix in the melted honey. At this point the peanut butter mixture should be a liquid consistency.

Use a spoon to transfer a small amount of the peanut butter mixture to the bottom of each silicone liner. Use the back of the spoon to spread the mixture across the bottom of each liner or swirl the liner until the bottom is evenly coated with the peanut butter mixture, about an 1/8 of an inch thick. Freeze the liners in the pan for 15 minutes or until set. While the peanut butter is setting, prepare the chocolate center.

Melt the chocolate chips and coconut milk in a double boiler over low heat or in a heatproof bowl set over a pan of gently simmering water. Stir frequently, using a rubber spatula, until the chocolate and coconut milk are completely melted and combined. Remove from heat and let cool until it's close to room temperature. If the chocolate mixture is too warm it will melt the peanut butter in the bottom of the liners. Once the chocolate has cooled down, remove the lined cupcake pan from the freezer. Use a spoon to transfer a dollop of chocolate, about the size of a tablespoon, into the center of each

peanut butter bottom, leaving room on the top and sides. Repeat this method for the remaining liners. Then use a spoon to pour the remaining peanut butter mixture into each liner, filling it and completely covering the sides and top of the chocolate center. Fill until the peanut butter mixture reaches about an 1/8 inch from the top of the liner. Freeze the completed pan for 20 minutes or until set.

An alternate method to make these cups would be to spoon about a tablespoon or so of the melted peanut butter mixture into each liner, one liner at a time. Pick up the liner and twirl it slowly in a circle, coating the bottom and sides evenly, about 3/4 of the way up the side of the liner, or use a spoon to pull the peanut butter mixture up the sides, evenly coating it. Freeze the completed pan for 10 minutes or until the peanut butter is set. Repeat this same process one more time to thicken the peanut butter coating. Once the chocolate mixture has cooled down, remove the pan from the freezer. Use a spoon to fill each peanut butter cup with the chocolate mixture. Fill to just below the peanut butter line, or about ⅛ inch below. Then use a spoon to pour and spread the remaining melted peanut butter mixture across the top of the chocolate center, even with the peanut butter line. Freeze the completed pan for 20 minutes or until set.

Remove the silicone liners. Enjoy right away or allow to thaw at room temperature for about 3-5 minutes. Store covered in the freezer for up to 1 month.

SERVES 4

Molten Chocolate Lava Cake

5 Tbsp (2 1/2 ounces) salted butter, plus more for greasing

1 cup (7 ounces) semisweet chocolate chips

2 large eggs

2 large egg yolks

3 Tbsp coconut sugar

1/4 tsp vanilla extract

2 Tbsp fine-ground blanched almond flour

1 heaping Tbsp cacao powder or unsweetened cocoa powder

1/8 tsp fine-grain sea salt

hot water for baking dish

cacao powder or unsweetened cocoa powder for garnish, optional

Grease the ramekins liberally with butter; set aside. Melt the chocolate chips and butter in the top pan of a double boiler over simmering water. Stir together until smooth and combined. Another method is to place the chocolate chips and butter in a large glass or metal mixing bowl set over a saucepan of simmering water. Stir intermittently, using a rubber spatula, until the chocolate and butter are completely melted and combined. Remove from the heat and let sit until the bowl is relatively cool to the touch. While the chocolate is cooling prepare other ingredients.

In a small bowl combine the almond flour, cacao powder, and salt. Use a fork to stir together until well combined; set aside.

In a large mixing bowl whisk together the eggs, egg yolks, coconut sugar, and vanilla until frothy. Use a rubber spatula to transfer and fold the chocolate into the egg and sugar mixture. Then sift the almond flour mixture into the chocolate and whisk until combined.

Pour the mixture evenly into ramekins. Tap lightly on the counter to remove air bubbles. Refrigerate uncovered for 30 minutes to set.

About 15 minutes before the 30 minutes is up, adjust oven rack to the middle position and preheat the oven to 425°F. Place the ramekins

into a 9"x13" baking dish and carefully pour hot water around the ramekins into the baking dish until it goes halfway up the sides of the ramekins. Bake for 15 to 18 minutes or until the edges look finished but the middle appears undone. Remove ramekins from the baking dish and let cool for at least 10 minutes. Slide a butter knife around the edge of the ramekin to pull the cake away from the sides, then turn it upside down over a plate and tap the bottom firmly until the cake slides out. Garnish with cocoa powder, raspberries or any other desired toppings. Store any leftovers in the refrigerator for up to a day, then reheat in the microwave for 30 seconds before eating.

MAKE AHEAD: Molten Chocolate Lava Cake batter – 1 week ahead, store in ramekin dishes. Cover with plastic wrap. Bake as needed.

YIELDS 1 LOAF

Pumpkin Bread

1 cup fine-ground blanched almond flour

1/4 cup coconut flour

1 tsp ground cinnamon

1/2 tsp baking soda

1/2 tsp fine-grain sea salt

1/2 tsp pumpkin pie spice

1/4 tsp ground cloves

1 cup coconut sugar

1/2 cup canned pumpkin puree

1/3 cup melted coconut oil

3 Tbsp canned full-fat coconut milk

1 vanilla bean, split lengthwise and seeds scraped, or 1 teaspoon vanilla extract

4 large eggs

Adjust an oven rack to the middle position. Preheat the oven to 325°F. Line the bottom of a 9"x 5" glass loaf pan with parchment paper; set aside.

Combine the almond flour, coconut flour, cinnamon, baking soda, salt, pumpkin pie spice, cloves, and coconut sugar in the bowl of a large food processor. Pulse 10 times or until mixed. Then add the wet ingredients: the pumpkin, coconut oil, coconut milk, vanilla bean seeds or extract, and eggs. Process for 30 seconds or until combined. Scrape down the sides and process again if needed.

Use a rubber spatula to transfer the mixture into the parchment-lined loaf pan. Bake for 70 to 75 minutes or until a toothpick inserted into the center comes out clean. Let cool for 15 minutes, then use a knife to loosen the bread from the sides of the pan. Remove the loaf from the pan by lifting the parchment paper. Let cool completely before slicing and serving.

NOTES: Glass pans and metal pans bake at different temperatures. If you only have a metal loaf pan to work with, try reducing the baking time to 45 to 50 minutes.

YIELDS 18 COOKIES

Simple Chocolate Chip Cookies

2 cups sifted fine-ground blanched almond flour

1 tsp baking soda

1/2 tsp fine-grain sea salt

1/3 cup raw honey

1/4 cup melted coconut oil

1 tsp vanilla extract

1 large egg, room temperature

1 cup (7 ounces) chocolate chips

Adjust an oven rack to the middle position. Preheat the oven to 350°F. Line two baking sheets with parchment paper or nonstick baking mats; set aside. (Note: If you're working with one baking sheet, allow to completely cool between batches.)

In a large mixing bowl, combine the almond flour, baking soda, and salt. Stir together using a fork until well combined.

In a separate medium-sized bowl, combine the honey, coconut oil, vanilla, and egg. Beat with an electric mixer on low speed until smooth. Add the honey mixture to the almond flour mixture and beat on low speed until combined.

Stir in chocolate chips. Use a small cookie scoop to transfer the dough evenly onto prepared baking sheets, about 2 inches apart or 9 cookies per baking sheet. If using one baking sheet, keep remaining uncooked dough refrigerated until ready to bake.

Bake each sheet separately on the middle rack at 350°F for 7 to 10 minutes or until the tops and edges are lightly browned. Once the cookies are done, remove the parchment or baking mat from the baking sheet and let cookies cool slightly before using a spatula to transfer them to a cooling rack. Store covered at room temperature for up to 3 days.

FINALE

Thanks so much for buying the All Star Real Food Cookbook. We are SO stoked to give you a peek into the kitchens and personalities behind some of the best real food chefs in the biz. Please make these meals and send us pictures, we'd love to see 'em. Make sure to tag the publishers (Paleo Treats) and use the hashtag **#allstarcookbook** so we can share the magic.

Enjoy good food!

Nik & Lee
Owners of Paleo Treats
Editors, All Star Real Food Cookbook